Selected Writings of

Alexander G. Wesman

1914 – 1973

Selected Writings of

Alexander G. Wesman

The Psychological Corporation

NEW YORK

Copyright © 1975 by The Psychological Corporation

Printed in the United States of America

ISBN: 0-15-003134-3

Library of Congress Catalog Card Number: 75-29766

Contents

Foreword

For thirty-five years Al Wesman's professional life was devoted to psychological tests. He studied them, he explained them, he taught others how to make them and, perhaps most important of all, he constantly tried to improve the use of them. He was actively engaged in test development and test publishing from 1938 to 1973, a period of enormous growth in the number and influence of tests in schools, psychological practice, and industry. In each of these areas he conducted research, produced finer instruments and fostered better understanding.

Although Wesman was a specialist in psychometrics, he was also a psychologist with broad interests in the field of human behavior. He felt that the skills of the testmaker should be used for the greater good of the examinee. An important step towards this goal was the education of the test user in the power, and also the limitations, of his testing tools. To this end he worked constantly, in talks and writings, and his judgment and advice were sought and valued. Since he was also an executive of a publishing house, Wesman's acceptance as an impartial expert by colleagues in competing houses as well as in academia reflects the esteem he had earned.

After obtaining B.S. and M.A. degrees from Fordham University, Wesman went to the World Book Company in 1938 as a research assistant. He left World Book to direct a comprehensive testing program in New York City schools from 1939 to 1941. He then joined the staff of the Graduate Record Examination, which at the time was a project of the Carnegie Foundation for the Advancement of Teaching, and subsequently became acting director of the GRE. When he left the GRE office in 1945, Wesman had gained significant experience in test construction, in dealing with committees to determine measurable objectives, and in helping college and university administrators interpret the results of tests. It was during this period, in 1944, that he also received his Ph.D. from Columbia University.

In 1945 Wesman joined The Psychological Corporation where he remained until his death in June 1973. It was at the Corporation that his abilities were fully realized. He became Director of the Test Division in 1965 and a Vice-president of the Corporation. He was co-author with George Bennett and Harold Seashore of what has become one of the most widely used and highly respected guidance batteries, the *Differential Aptitude Tests*. He was also author or co-author of several other published instruments: the *Personnel Classification Test*, the *Personnel Tests for Industry*, the *College Qualification Tests*, and the *Academic Promise Tests*. He wrote many articles and was greatly in demand as a speaker on measurement techniques and measurement philosophy. In Wesman's professional work these characteristics of the man are apparent: He was a first-rate craftsman in measurement, he could communicate lucidly and effectively with a wide range of people from the technical specialist to the unsophisticated test user, and he was deeply concerned with furthering the proper uses of measurement.

Wesman's skill in working with people was recognized and honored by his colleagues. He served on professional committees and contributed to important reports issued by some of these groups. For five years he was a Trustee and examining member of the American Board of Examiners of Professional Psychology. He was Secretary, from 1954 to 1957, of the American Psychological Association's Division of Evaluation and Measurement and President of that Division in 1966-67. He was a Fellow, too, of APA's Divisions of Industrial Psychology and Counseling Psychology.

In tribute to the memory of Al Wesman this collection of some of his published works has been prepared. It reflects his work and thoughts on a variety of topics over the years. The style of writing is remarkably clear and the substance always merits attention. A complete list of his publications begins on page 175.

Just as two dimensions can never fully describe a three-dimensional object, neither can a paper tribute adequately describe Al Wesman. He was a kind person who genuinely liked people. He was interested in and helpful to people at all levels and they reciprocated his sincere concern. Those who knew him only slightly were saddened by his untimely death. To those of us who knew him well his death was a profound loss. It is a privilege to be able to offer this recognition of his work.

Jerome E. Doppelt
James H. Ricks, Jr.

The Psychological Corporation
June 1975

Selected Writings of

Alexander G. Wesman

The Usefulness of Correctly Spelled Words in a Spelling Test

One of the difficulties met in the construction of spelling tests of the recognition type is the difference in the validity of the item in its correct and incorrect forms. For example, in the spelling section of the Bennett Stenographic Aptitude Test, words which are correctly spelled as presented are not included in the scoring because these words were found ineffective. Only those words which are presented wrongly spelled contribute to the testee's score. This procedure results in decreased efficiency of the test, since only half the items presented (fifty of one hundred) are actually used. The remaining items represent merely a necessary 'padding' for the misspelled words.

It is desirable for a test to have maximum efficiency. This can be accomplished by maximizing the reliability of every item. For the type of test under consideration it would involve:

(a) Maximizing the reliability of the misspelled words;
(b) Maximizing the reliability of the correctly spelled words.

Since step 'a' is ordinarily observed in test construction, it is step 'b' which is more promising for improvement of present instruments of this nature. Maximizing the reliability of the correctly spelled words means the discovery, by experimentation, of appropriate words which will be effective test items when presented in their correctly spelled form. The technique described herein is one method of such experimentation.

The technique used to obtain the desired result—a fully efficient spelling test of the true-false type—is relatively simple; however, since the author has found no reference in the literature to its previous use, it is reported herewith.

From *Journal of Educational Psychology*, 1946, 37, 242-246. Copyright 1946 by the American Psychological Association. Reprinted by permission.

The author wished to construct two equivalent one hundred-item forms of a spelling test which would be efficient tests. He judged that he would need to start with a pool of three hundred items in order to have at least two hundred useful items for the two final forms of the test. A group of three hundred commonly misspelled words was selected from Gates' *A List of Spelling Difficulties in 3876 Words,* and the most frequent error form of each word was noted. Words were chosen from the top grade placement of Gates' list (grade 8.0 and up) because of the intended level of the tests to be constructed. The three hundred words selected were then used to make two tests, each of three hundred items. Each test had half its items correctly spelled, and the other half of its items incorrectly spelled according to the most frequent error form noted in Gates. The tests were in a sense 'mirrors' of each other, since a word spelled properly in one form was improperly spelled in the other form of the test.

The tests were administered to the entire ninth grade of a junior high school (ninety-three boys and one hundred nine girls), half the students taking each form of the test. The two forms were similarly administered to the entire eleventh and twelfth grades of a senior high school containing eighty-one boys and one hundred seventeen girls. No attempt was made to analyze the data separately by sex.

Coefficients of correlation of each item against the total score on the test were obtained for each word in its correctly and incorrectly spelled form. These coefficients were determined separately for the junior and senior high school students. The highest-scoring twenty-seven per cent and lowest-scoring twenty-seven per cent on total score in each school group were selected as criterion groups. The per cent of the upper group which passed each item was compared with the per cent of the lower group passing that item. These values were then referred to Flanagan's chart and the appropriate coefficient was found therein. Thus, four coefficients were obtained for each of the three hundred words:[1] (1) when correctly spelled with ninth-grade students; (2) when correctly spelled with eleventh- and twelfth-grade students; (3) when misspelled with ninth-grade students; and (4) when misspelled with eleventh- and twelfth-grade students.

Table I presents distributions of correlation coefficients under the four conditions, together with the median and the quartile deviation of each distribution. Inspection of the table reveals that higher coefficients are obtained, on the average, with the incorrectly spelled forms of the words. The median coefficients for misspelled forms of the words are .50 and .51 for the junior and senior high school groups, respectively, as compared with medians of .38 and .34 for the correctly spelled forms. The variabil-

---

[1] Because of typing errors, two words were incorrectly spelled in both forms, and one word was correctly spelled on both forms.

TABLE I. Distributions of Correlation Coefficients of Misspelled and Correctly Spelled Forms of Words for Ninth-Grade and Eleventh- and Twelfth-Grade Pupils

r	Misspelled		Correctly Spelled	
	9th Grade N = 202	11th & 12th Grades N = 198	9th Grade N = 202	11th & 12th Grades N = 198
.84–.89	1	2	0	0
.78–.83	13	8	1	0
.72–.77	16	16	8	3
.66–.71	27	29	14	11
.60–.65	39	35	14	13
.54–.59	32	34	20	7
.48–.53	37	46	29	33
.42–.47	20	32	43	32
.36–.41	27	22	30	36
.30–.35	25	24	34	29
.24–.29	22	16	26	41
.18–.23	11	12	20	17
.12–.17	10	7	23	14
.06–.11	8	8	6	14
.00–.05	3	5	21	34
Negative coefficients −.01––.39	10	5	10	15
Total	301	301	299	299
Median	.50	.51	.38	.34
Q	.15	.14	.14	.14

ity of the coefficients is relatively constant for all four conditions, the respective quartile deviations being .15, .14, .14, and .14.

The data in Table I are in accord with previous experience that misspelled words are generally more discriminating. This is further confirmed by Table II, which shows the number of words which have higher coefficients for both school groups when misspelled, the number which are higher for a single group, and the number which are equal or lower in both groups.[2] Slightly more than half the words used have higher coefficients for the misspelled form at both grade levels, as against only thirty-one which are lower at both levels. This superiority of the misspelled words is emphasized when the individual grade levels are considered.

---

[2] Three words are excluded from Table II: the two which were misspelled, and the one which was correctly spelled in both forms.

TABLE II. A Comparison of the Item-Test Correlation of 297 Words as Presented in Misspelled and Correctly Spelled Form

	9th Grade	11th and 12th Grades	Both Grades
r higher when misspelled	196	218	153
r equal	4	5	0
r higher when correctly spelled	97	74	31

These data throw light on the relative usefulness of misspelled and correctly spelled words, to the advantage of the misspelled. From the test construction standpoint, however, it is equally important to note that there are a large number of words which are useful when correctly spelled. As shown in Table I, one hundred ninety-three of the correctly spelled words have item-test score coefficients of .30 or higher at the ninth-grade level, and one hundred sixty-four of these words have coefficients of that magnitude at the eleventh- and twelfth-grade level. Their use in a true-false spelling test would represent a real contribution to the test's efficiency rather than acting as merely 'padding.'

It is not here proposed that the best way to measure spelling ability is by means of the true-false recognition type of item. The answer to that question depends on the aspect of spelling ability to be measured, or the use for which spelling ability is intended. There are purposes (e.g., proof-reading) for which the recognition type of item is best suited.

It is probable that the use of this 'mirror' technique for such tests will enable other test constructors to find words which will be useful for their own specific applications.

A useful study, or series of studies, might well be undertaken to determine the most desirable proportions of misspelled and correctly spelled words to include in a test of this sort. For obvious practical reasons, a test consisting entirely of misspelled words would not be feasible. The best proportion, however, should be subject to experimental determination.

References

1. Bennett, George K. *Stenographic Aptitude Test, Manual of Directions.* New York: The Psychological Corporation, 1945.

2. Flanagan, John C. *A Table of the Values of the Product Moment Coefficient of Correlation in a Normal Bivariate Population Corresponding to Given Proportions of Successes.* New York: Coöperative Test Service, 1936.

3. Gates, Arthur I. *A List of Spelling Difficulties in 3876 Words.* New York: Bureau of Publications, Teachers College, 1937. Pp. 166.

The Validation
of Intelligence Tests

The validity of an intelligence test is difficult to assess—much more so than tests designed to measure some special aptitude, which need only be checked against actual later performance. No single clear-cut experiment can prove the real worth and limitations of any test of general mental ability. In the final analysis, its validity rests on the validity of the basic philosophy underlying the test and the extent to which the test's content faithfully exemplifies that philosophy.

Two of the most frequently used procedures for establishing the validity of a new intelligence test are to correlate it with previous measures of intelligence, and to observe the way in which it differentiates between groups judged to differ in intelligence.

The correlation coefficients obtained in pursuing the former method have some value as contributory evidence, and it is desirable for a number of reasons that they be reported. That they are not, taken alone, clear-cut evidence of validity becomes apparent as soon as one asks, "How large should such coefficients be?" Obviously, they ought not to be extremely low, since that would indicate that the new test is not measuring the same general functions as the previously-established tests. On the other hand, they should not be too high, since extremely high coefficients would indicate that the new test is essentially duplicating the measurements of the previously-established test, and consequently represents no advance in the field of mental measurement.[1]

From *Manual for the Personnel Classification Test*, 1947 edition, published by The Psychological Corporation.

[1] This statement does not hold, of course, for tests designed only to save time or cost by quicker measurement, as in abbreviated or separate-answer-sheet modifications of established tests. In such cases, the philosophy underlying the established test is accepted *in toto*, and

5

In the latter method, it is necessary first to decide on some basis for believing that one group is more intelligent or possesses higher mental ability than another. With tests intended primarily for use in schools, the groups are ordinarily pupils at various grade levels or at various age levels. Much can be said in justification of this approach. It may be noted, however, that those tests which are most like achievement tests in school subject matter tend to be the most successful in their differentiation between successive grade levels. While a large amount of school-subject content may be desirable for some purposes, it naturally limits the usefulness of the test for groups either no longer in school or following different courses of study.

The use of the successive age approach is of dubious worth in the validation of an intelligence test intended primarily (or even incidentally) for use with adults. For one thing, experimental evidence is contradictory as to the age up to which intelligence continues growing; apparently the experimental conclusions depend at least partially on the type of test used in the experiment. A second source of confusion is the greater average education of younger adults as compared with older men and women. More people have had more schooling in recent years, a fact which may or may not result in their being really more intelligent, but which may be expected to result in higher intelligence test scores. How much higher would depend on such factors as how similar the test content is to school subject matter, how accustomed the adults are to taking objective tests, how heavily sheer speed counts in the test score, and the like.

Study of the test's differentiation between adult groups with varying amounts of education is somewhat more profitable. This approach is based on the assumption that, under our educational system, the more intelligent individuals go farther in school or college, obtaining more education on the average than the less intelligent. This may be due to self-selection, in that the more intelligent *wanted* more education; or it may have been circumstantial selection, such as that of colleges accepting for admission only the more intelligent, and that of actual failure at various school levels; or it may result from any of several other kinds of selection. It would be naive to believe that these selection processes operate perfectly for all individuals – of course, they do not; however, it is highly probable that they operate *on the average*, when sizable groups with various educational backgrounds can be compared.

A similar approach is the comparison of groups of adults assumed to differ in intelligence by reason of their job levels or professional status. The

---

the parent test acts as the "perfect criterion." Such shortened tests should have as high correlation as can be obtained with the parent test; they represent useful efforts toward quicker or easier measurement, but not fundamentally improved ways of measuring mental function.

assumption here is that the more intelligent will attain positions of greater responsibility or greater complexity.

From a practical standpoint, some of the most valuable evidence of an intelligence test's validity is its ability to predict success in jobs requiring intelligence. If intelligence were the only quality necessary for success, this type of evidence by itself could be accepted as the only demonstration of validity needed, so far as a specific organization considering the use of the test is concerned. But, inasmuch as other abilities or personal traits are also required ordinarily, the test's ability to predict cannot usually be judged or used in so simple a way.

Because intelligence is but one factor among several, it is desirable to use a *critical score* evaluation of the test rather than a correlation coefficient in judging the validity of the test in a business or industrial situation. One frequently finds, in analyzing job requirements, that a certain minimum amount of intelligence is necessary for successful performance on a given job, but that varying amounts above that minimum are of relatively little importance compared with other qualities. For example, in many sales jobs the salesman needs enough mental ability to understand his product and selling technique and to know what sales approach his competition uses. In a large group of successful salesmen, it will be found that almost all of them have at least that much intelligence. This does not necessarily mean that the most intelligent will be the most successful. Among the men who have the minimum required intelligence, the most successful salesmen will probably be those who are superior in other personal qualities. The intelligence test should therefore be used simply to discover whether or not the prospective salesman has the minimum required intelligence; scores far above the minimum need not be looked on more favorably than scores little above the minimum. It is even true, in some instances, that too high a score should be regarded unfavorably as a possible indication that the applicant will not long remain content with his position and will require promotion more rapidly than the organization is prepared to advance him.

The desired minimum score is the critical score. It may be found by obtaining the scores of successful and unsuccessful men on the job, and locating that score above which almost all the successful men fall and below which most unsuccessful men are found. Each organization should set its own critical score for applicants for each type of position for which testing is part of the hiring procedure. The usefulness of the test should be judged by the extent to which it can thus separate successful from unsuccessful employees.

Active versus Blank Responses
to Multiple-Choice Items

In the process of constructing multiple-choice tests, one is sometimes forced to decide whether to require the subject to mark every possible response or whether to require him to mark only choices of a given category. For example, we may have a spelling test in which the subject is required to mark only those words which have been wrongly spelled, or we may require him to mark every word as being correct or incorrect. In the first instance, we consider all blank responses as indicating the subject's judgment that these words are properly spelled. In the second instance, we evaluate only his active responses.

The blank response form is probably to be preferred on the basis of the time factor; more items can be answered in a given period of time when only some items require an active response than when all items require marking. The speed advantage will vary according to the complexity of response required and test format. If the marking is simple, the advantage will be relatively small; whereas, if the marking is complicated, the advantage of the blank response form may be appreciable.

The blank response form has at least one disadvantage which may outweigh the advantage of its permitting greater speed. This is the confusion which frequently results from our inability to know whether the blank response really represents a judgment by the subject, or whether it is merely an 'omit.' This difficulty is absent only in a pure 'power' test, when everyone has all the time he needs for every item. To the extent that speed is a factor in the test performance, the confusion element becomes increasingly important. If a subject does not finish the test, it is difficult to assign an equitable score. For example, let us suppose that the spelling test mentioned above has fifty words and the subject has marked the fortieth word as being incorrect, leaving the last ten words unmarked. Unless we are sure he has had enough time to finish the test, we do not know whether he looked at any or all of the last ten words and considered them as being properly spelled. If we assign a score on the basis of the first forty words only, and he has really made judgments about some or all of the remaining ten words, he is being penalized unfairly if more than five of the last ten words are truly correctly spelled, or not being penalized adequately if fewer than five are correctly spelled. Similarly, if we assign his score on the basis of all fifty items, and he has actually not looked past the fortieth item, he is penalized unfairly or rewarded unfairly depending on the number of correctly spelled words among the last ten items of the test.

Theoretically, we may expect that, since the active response form eliminates the ambiguity of the blank response form, there should result a greater reliability. The study reported here is an investigation of the validity of this hypothesis.

The test used consisted of fifty sentences, each sentence being divided into five parts (items). The subject was required to decide whether each part of each sentence was grammatically correct, or whether one or more of the parts were wrong. Two forms of the test were available. They were administered to two hundred ninety-nine ninth-grade high-school students.[1] Form A was administered first, with instructions to one hundred seventy of the students (Group I) to mark every part 'Right' or 'Wrong' on a special answer sheet. The one hundred twenty-nine students in Group II were instructed only to pick out those sentence parts which were 'Wrong,' and mark those responses on an appropriate answer sheet. Form B was then administered to these two groups, but with reversed directions: Group I now was instructed to mark 'Wrong' parts only; Group II marked every sentence part as 'Right' or 'Wrong.'

The per cent passing each item (each sentence part) was found. Since there were fifty sentences and five parts to a sentence in each form, it was necessary to compute 1000 per cent passing values. This number is too large to present for meaningful comparisons. Accordingly, the five per cents for each sentence for each form were averaged. The average per cent passing was: Form A, active response, sixty-seven per cent; Form A, blank response, seventy per cent; Form B, active response, sixty per cent; Form B, blank response, seventy-eight per cent.

On the whole, the items seem to be a little more difficult under the active response condition; i.e., when the subject is asked to mark both 'rights' and 'wrongs.' The greater difference in mean per cent passing on Form B than on Form A may result from a combination of the following:

---

[1]The author is indebted to Leslie O. Johnson, Principal, The High School, Gloucester, Massachusetts, for the testing of these students.

1) there is a real difference in difficulty between the two forms;[2] 2) the transition from marking 'wrongs' only to marking both 'rights' and 'wrongs,' and *vice versa*, may result in negative transfer in marking Form B, which was the second test taken. As for the difference in means within each form under the two experimental conditions, the active form of response may actually increase the difficulty of the items; or the greater time required by the active form may prevent more subjects from reaching the last items of the test, and thus serve artificially to make those items appear more difficult. To investigate the latter hypothesis, distributions were made of last item attempted (as judged by positive marks on the answer sheets). The data are presented in Table I, and reveal that the active response was

TABLE I. Last Item Completed under Active and Blank Response Conditions

Last Item Completed	Form A		Form B	
	Active Response	Blank Response	Active Response	Blank Response
49–50	28%	56%	21%	76%
40–48	39%	21%	34%	19%
Below 40	33%	23%	45%	5%
N	170	129	136	165

indeed more time-consuming and actually did not permit as many subjects to reach the last items of the test. As further verification, the average per cent passing was computed for the first twenty-five and last twenty-five sentences separately. Table II presents these means, and confirms the fact that it is the failure of subjects to reach the last items that is responsible for the smaller per cent passing on the active form of the test. The differences in means are much larger for the second half of the test than for the first.

'Per cent passing' in this study was calculated as the proportion of the entire group taking the test which answered an item correctly. The observed per cents would increase if only those actually reacting to each item were used as the base for computation. This analysis was not attempted because it would require guessing as to whether, under blank response conditions, the subjects had looked at one or more items after the last one marked and found no errors in grammar, or whether failure to mark the items was truly an indication that those items had not been read.

---

[2] The author has evidence from another study that, by roughly twelve points in score, Form B is actually somewhat more difficult than Form A.

TABLE II. Average Per Cent Passing First and Second Twenty-five Sentences under Active and Blank Response Conditions

	Form A		Form B	
	Active Response	Blank Response	Active Response	Blank Response
Sentences 1–25	83%	78%	79%	86%
Sentences 26–50 ...	51%	62%	40%	71%

Item-test correlation coefficients were computed for Forms A and B of the test under active and blank response conditions by use of upper and lower twenty-seven per cent groups and the Flanagan chart.[3] The average item-test coefficients were: Form A, active response, .41; Form A, blank response, .25; Form B, active response, .35; Form B, blank response, .25. With both forms, the average item-test r is higher under the active response condition than under the blank response condition.

It would be possible for this superiority of the active response condition to be the result of the same factor which caused apparent increased difficulty; namely, the relatively few subjects answering the last items of the test. This hypothesis can be tested. It is presumed that some imperfect but positive relationship exists between the subject's competence in the content of the test and his speed of response to the items; i.e., there is a tendency for the better subjects to answer more items. Therefore, these better subjects will reach and correctly answer some of the items near the end of the test, while poorer subjects (many of whom might have answered the items correctly) do not reach these items. To the degree that these items are easy, the result is artificially high item-test coefficients.

To discover whether this would account for the result cited above, average item-test coefficients were computed for the first twenty-five and last twenty-five sentences separately. The data are presented in Table III, and reveal that there is almost certainly an artificial character in the item-test r's for the last items under the active response condition. Nevertheless, the average item-test r is higher even for the first twenty-five sentences under the active response condition. Apparently, requiring active responses does improve item-test correlation somewhat.

What effect has the use of one or the other type of response on the reliability and validity of the test? The strong probability is that validity will

[3]Flanagan, J.C. *A table of the values of the product moment coefficient of correlation in a normal bivariate population corresponding to given proportions of successes.* New York: Cooperative Test Service, 1936.

TABLE III. Average Item-Test Coefficients for First and Second Twenty-five Sentences under Active and Blank Response Conditions

	Form A		Form B	
	Active Response	Blank Response	Active Response	Blank Response
Sentences 1–25....	.27	.25	.33	.24
Sentences 26–50...	.55	.25	.37	.26

not be affected, except insofar as validity is dependent on reliability. At least the content of the test is the same under both active and blank response conditions. No outside criterion was available which would permit investigation of this question. The reliability of the test, on the other hand, might be expected to vary with the type of response used. Since more subjects answer a larger number of items where they are asked to mark wrong items only, this blank response condition results effectively in a longer test than the active response situation. This greater effective length of test makes for additional reliability. However, the individual items should be more reliable when active responses are required for all items, and this greater individual item reliability should summate to increased test reliability. Which force (if either) is the more effective in the experimental situation?

Coefficients of correlation between odd and even halves of each form of the test under each response condition were computed for boys and girls separately and combined. The corrected (by Spearman-Brown formula) coefficients are shown in Table IV. These coefficients are somewhat spuriously high of course, since the tests had an element of speed involved; and since speed was a more important factor under the active response condition, the coefficients are probably more spurious for that response than for the blank condition. Critical ratios of differences in the coefficients were computed, using the Fisher z function.

There appears to be no real difference, in reliability, between the active and blank conditions. The one critical ratio which approaches statistical significance (2.50 for total group, Form A) applies to an instance in which the active response coefficient is higher. Since it is only one difference out of six, and since (as indicated above) there is more spurious magnification in the active response test coefficient, the evidence can only be accepted as showing no real difference.

If the results of this experiment are typical for situations in which one is faced with the choice of using active or blank responses, the choice would seemingly depend on mechanical advantages in a specific situation rather

TABLE IV.* Reliability Coefficients and Critical Ratios under Active and Blank Response Conditions

	Form A						Form B					
	Boys		Girls		Boys and Girls		Boys		Girls		Boys and Girls	
	r_{11}	N	r_{11}	N	r_{11}	N	r_{11}	N	r_{11}	N	r_{11}	N
Active	.88	53	.93	117	.92	170	.88	91	.90	45	.89	136
Blank	.86	83	.89	46	.86	129	.86	55	.91	110	.89	165
CR	.45		1.32		2.50		.48		.30		0	

*The reliability coefficients are the odd-even correlations stepped up by the Spearman-Brown formula. The CR was obtained by converting r to Fisher's z-function and getting ratio of difference between z's to standard error of difference.

than on any inherent superiority of measurement. For equal testing time the theoretical advantages of greater sampling under the blank condition, and lesser ambiguity of interpretation (and consequent item reliability) of the active condition, seem to equal each other. The appropriate considerations for reaching a decision in a specific situation will probably depend on such factors as the desired magnitude of range in raw scores, the applicability of one form or the other to mechanical aids such as standard IBM answer sheets, the relative difficulty of writing simple instructions for the population for which the test is intended, the scoring problem, etc.

The writer is aware that it is dangerous to generalize from a single experiment. Variations in population and test content might produce different results from those reported herein. The present study does serve, however, to demonstrate the greater danger of making decisions regarding item types on the basis of armchair logic, and the need of exposing hypotheses concerning items to experimental investigation.

Needed: More Understanding
of Present Tests

There is a well-recognized need for the invention of psychological tests which will yield objective valid measurements in areas which have heretofore been untouched, or in areas which are now represented only by woefully inadequate instruments. Tests predictive of executive ability, selling ability, creativity in painting and sculpture, literary composition, teaching skill, conscientiousness, preservation, and research ingenuity are but a few of those which education and industry could profitably utilize. No remarks which follow are intended to discourage anyone who has found a way to probe these abilities or any of the hundreds of others which have thus far eluded test construction. The burden of the present argument is not that we do not need new tests, — but rather that we need to know more about the instruments already available to us.

All of the points I shall make in this paper will probably be matters of common knowledge to some of you; perhaps some of my remarks will be superfluous for all of this audience. I am nevertheless prompted to provide these reminders of good test procedures because they are so frequently neglected in published research papers and published tests. It is my belief that one of the important functions which the membership of our Association serves is that of reminding or informing researchers in education of some of these principles.

What Is Meant by Validity?

Unlike a popular quiz show, I shall start, rather than end, with the $64 question — validity. The word "validity" has become so much a part of our everyday discourse, that we rarely halt our thought stream long

From *Improving Educational Research*, 1948 Official Report, American Educational Research Association.

enough to inquire "validity for what?" Doubtless the Wechsler-Bellevue test is a valid measure of intelligence; so is the Otis; so also are the Alpha tests, the Pintner tests, the Thurstone tests of Primary Mental Abilities. They are not equally valid, to be sure. How could they be, since they are measuring different things. Each is a test of intelligence, but it is more — it is in and of itself a definition of intelligence, and these definitions vary from test to test.

How valid each test is depends on two considerations: whether you agree with the definition of intelligence as represented by the content of the test, and what you are trying to predict. If a given kind of learning is what you are trying to predict (and the ability to learn is certainly one good definition of intelligence), then that test is most valid which best predicts the given kind of learning. The validity of a test is always specific to a situation; a "generally" valid test is one which is satisfactorily valid in a large number of specific situations.

The same considerations which determine the validity of intelligence tests also determine the validity of achievement tests: what specific ability we are trying to evaluate, and whether we agree that the test's content satisfactorily taps that ability. What is the validity of a spelling test? We need to define spelling, just as we needed to define intelligence, before we can judge validity. What kind of spelling ability are we interested in? Is it the ability to single out incorrectly spelled words, as a proof-reader or editor needs to do? If so, our test should be one that provides direct evidence of that skill. Or is it the ability to recall correct spellings of words for creative writing? In that case, the spelling test should tap that specific skill. It may be proposed, and quite legitimately, that the two kinds of spelling tests would correlate highly. Nevertheless, it has not been demonstrated, so far as the writer knows, that the correlation (even when corrected for attenuation) would be perfect. Since the skills are different, the difference should be taken into account when selecting the test to be used in a specific situation.

What has been said for spelling is equally applicable to every other achievement area. The student who can best reproduce the formal theorems of a geometry text is not always one who can apply the principles of that discipline to problem situations. Our selection of tests to evaluate geometry achievement should be conditioned by the goals we have set for the geometry course.

The importance of scrutinizing test content for appropriateness to the specific situation is ignored with appalling frequency. For several years it was one of my responsibilities to explain the nature and purposes of the Graduate Record Examination. Time and again, I was asked by an institution to advise it on how to revamp its curriculum to result in higher scores by the students on this examination. My reply, framed with such tact as I could command, was that the institution had no moral right to make such a change, unless the faculty had first examined its own broad philosophy of education and the specific goals which derived from it, scrutinized the detailed content of the Graduate Record Examination, and decided that either the Examination adequately exemplified that philosophy and those goals, or that the Examination's objectives were more acceptable to that institution than its own. Unless one of these two judgments had been made, the institution must regard the Examination as only partly valid for its purposes — valid only to the extent that the Examination conformed to the ideas and needs of that school.

This same principle holds for elementary- and secondary-school levels as well. The better achievement batteries, such as the Stanford and Metropolitan Tests, are constructed with considerable thought to inclusion of important educational concepts and skills. Curriculums are inspected and subjectmatter experts are consulted to assure representativeness and significance in the test materials. Doubtless many (perhaps even most) school systems find these batteries to be adequate reflections of their own goals. Where this is so, well and good. There are at the same time sufficient differences among school systems so that for some the batteries will not reflect what they are trying to teach. For such systems, the tests can be only partially valid. Each system has the obligation to make the required judgments for its own situation.

The necessity of keeping the criterion clearly in mind is perhaps most obvious when we use aptitude tests. Here it should be crystal-clear that we need always to ask: Aptitude for what? Is a test of mechanical comprehension likely to predict equally well success in an engineering course, in a drafting course, in jobs such as armature winder, maintenance mechanic, navigator, or bus driver? The answer is obviously "No." It is, perhaps, less obvious that the test will not predict equally well success as maintenance mechanic in two different plants. The equipment to be serviced and the responsibilities in the two plants may be so different that the test is quite valid in one situation while being invalid in the other.

If we recognize the specificity of validity, it should be apparent that there is no excuse for talking about *the* validity of a test, or for reporting *the* validity coefficient. There is no such thing as *the* validity; there are validity coefficients obtained under specific circumstances for specific populations. The most important validation in any given instance is local validation by the test user for his own particular purposes. Next in importance is validation in a similar situation elsewhere. What we need for every test is as many coefficients as we can practically gather, together with a detailed description of the population from which each is derived. The test user can seek out the population which most resembles his own, and make a reasonable guess as to the probable validity of the test for the group with which he is concerned.

What Is Reliability?

Despite constant exhortation by psychometricians, we still find references in conversation, in research studies, and in test manuals to *the* reliability of a test. The dependence of the size of an obtained reliability coefficient on the population from which it was determined is a basic concept in the field of tests and measurement. Yet we still find considerable variation in practice of reporting these coefficients. One might take, for example, the November-December issue of the *Journal of Consulting Psychology*, which came to my desk while this statement was being written. This journal reports new tests as they arrive in the offices of the editor. The variability in reporting coefficients is almost complete — from total absence of coefficients to detailed descriptions of the populations for which coefficients are presented. That the variability is not the result of any lack of sensitivity to such figures on the part of the *Journal's* editor can be readily ascertained by examination of the published manuals.

While we are on this topic of reliability, one or two other common misinterpretations of test data might well be noted. Many tests give adequate data concerning total test scores, but report part scores without accompanying reliability coefficients. This practice is unfortunate, if not downright misleading. The less sophisticated user is very likely to assume part scores to be about as reliable as the total scores. This is sometimes true; more often, it is not. The act of reporting a part score bears the implication that the author intends the part score for use. If it is to be used, some evidence should be presented as to its reliability under various circumstances.

A more complex ramification of assumed reliability occurs in the treatment of differences between part scores. All too few test users — psychologists and educators alike — are seemingly aware that the difference between two scores (or part scores) is less reliable than either of the scores (or parts). Important decisions are made daily regarding a student's relative ability in two subjectmatter fields, or two aptitudes, on the basis of unreliable differences. Authors who want users of their tests to make such judgments on the basis of part scores should fulfil their obligations by reporting data concerning the reliability of score differences. Lest my educational colleagues think I am singling them out for disapproval, I might say that the misuse of part score differences on the Wechsler-Bellevue by clinical psychologists is a matter of grave concern to many of us just now.

Another source of confusion with respect to reliability that needs to be eliminated is the type of reliability coefficient reported. Consider particularly the use of split-half (usually odd-even) coefficients with tests in which speed plays an important role. The impropriety of this practice has been noted by every good book in the field of psychometrics; despite which, authors blithely proceed to cite these entirely spurious coefficients to demonstrate the pretended excellence of their tests. For many years, the most widely used clerical test presented such a coefficient. The remarkable and regrettable fact is that during that period not a single user of the test protested to the publisher. The reference was only deleted when we ourselves noted the coefficient and removed it in a revision of the manual.

As a demonstration of the spuriousness of split-half coefficients, the authors of the Differential Aptitude Tests present in their manual a table comparing these coefficients with test-retest coefficients for the same populations. With the ninth-grade boys, as one instance, Forms A and B correlate .83; the respective split-half coefficients are .990 and .996. Of the twenty split-half coefficients, computed, the lowest was .97 and the highest was .998.

Sex is another source of confusion and mispractice with respect to reliability. Actually, it is simply a special case under the principle of homogeneous vs. heterogeneous grouping. Because it is so often not recognized as such, it deserves special attention. Whether because of inherited biological characteristics or cultural pressures, there are many areas in which boys are superior to girls, and vice versa. To use them as a single population is improper. As an example, let us cite data from the Mechanical Reasoning Test of the Differential Aptitude Test series. For a group of twelfth-grade girls, the obtained reliability coefficient was .69. When, for the purposes of this paper, the boys and girls were thrown into a single distribution, the resulting coefficient was .87. This is obviously a serious divergence in terms of our confidence in the stability of the girls' scores. An author is always under obligation to investigate whether important sex differences occur with his test and to present his data appropriately.

What about the Norms of Tests?

The differentiation of sex groups is also important in the presentation of norms. Where sex differences are considerable, as in the example just cited, there is little justification for presenting norms tables based on combined sex groups. If one does so, a score which is poor within the better sex group will seem relatively good compared with standard score or percentile norms from a combined distribution. Since, for such abilities as mechanical reasoning, a boy's competition will come largely from boys, his scores should be compared with those of boys rather than with a meaningless nonsex-differentiated distribution. As an illustration a twelfth-grade boy scoring 35 on the Mechanical Reasoning Test of the Differential Aptitude Test series would be at the fifty-fourth percentile in a distribution based on both sexes; when compared with boys only, he is at the twenty-second percentile.

The entire matter of norms needs careful review in the thinking of many test users. The value of representative, nationwide norms has been fairly well impressed on our consciousness, and some very ambitious standardization programs have been conducted — most notably, perhaps, by the publishers of the Stanford and Metropolitan Achievement Tests. Not nearly so well appreciated have been the importance of local norms, and the desirability of presenting norms for as many different, carefully defined groups as we can get. The more relevant frames of reference we can make available, the more closely we can define the competition of a specific individual, class or school, the richer will be the interpretation of test scores.

The fact that norms are supposed to help us locate the person tested along a sensible continuum is sometimes ignored. A notable illustration of this weakness appears in the manual for a popular personality test. This instrument proposes, on the basis of responses to 180 yes-no questions, to yield twelve separate, reliable, meaningful adjustment scores. Each score is consequently based on exactly fifteen questions. Aside from the obvious unreliability of the inventory, it is interesting to see how the test's own norms reveal the preposterousness of this fond hope. Thus a score of nine on the self-reliance scale places you at the twenty-fifth percentile; make three more correct responses on this scale and you find yourself at the seventy-fifth percentile. Quite a jump! On this same scale, a score of one is no better than a score of four — in each case, you are still at the first percentile. Nonetheless, this test is currently in widespread use.

Another aspect of the interpretation of norms, which is especially important with personality tests, concerns the factor of motivation. Norms obtained in a counseling situation cannot be expected to hold up in a selection situation. A voluntary clinical patient can be persuaded that it is to his interest to answer the questions honestly. The motivation of an applicant for college admission or for employment will result in a strong tendency to make the best possible score; the attitude of a reluctant selectee for the armed services is a horse of still a different color. It is naive to expect that responses of the subjects will have the same meaning under these several conditions. Not only the norms, but reliability and validity, will obviously be affected by the subject's motivation.

What Can We Do about It?

The differences between what we know to be good test practice and what is frequently done are so many that considerably more time would be required to note them than either you or I are prepared to spend here. Such topics as the overlap between intelligence, achievement and aptitude tests, and the overlap of each of them with school grades; the need for keeping norms up to date because of shifting populations; the relationship between speed in a test and the nature of the function it is intended to measure; the difference between using single test items of survey tests as clues for investigation and as a basis for diagnosis and remedial action — these and similar areas of inadequate understanding by many test users might well provide material for a paper as long as the present one. I think, however, I have already demonstrated the validity of my thesis — that tests now available and in widespread use need to be better understood and better used.

The question is: What shall we, who are better informed, do about it? Four courses of action may be proposed:

1. Encourage the publication of far more research data relating to tests. Much valuable information is lost because test users do not make their data available to others. More publication in journals might well be encouraged to add to our store of reliability coefficients, validity coefficients and norms. Those who have the data should be made aware that even in physical science research, confirmation of previous results is important — the results need not be new to represent a contribution to the field. Where, for one reason or other, the user is reluctant to publish the data himself, he should be urged to submit them to the test publishers for information and dissemination.

2. Call weaknesses in specific tests to the attention of the publisher. If the deficiency is inadvertent, the publisher should be grateful to have it brought to his attention so that he can take steps to correct it. In any event, he should be made aware of your disapproval as a direct means of influencing his future conduct.

3. In writing books or treatises dealing with tests, write critically. Authors should recognize their obligations to their readers to evaluate carefully any tests which are mentioned. The magic of the printed word is sufficient even for intelligent audiences so that tests which are merely named are accepted as being good. If it is inappropriate to evaluate the tests named in a book, then only those tests which the author esteems most highly should be included.

4. Finally, put your money where your faith is. Do not buy tests which you know to be inferior, or for which insufficient or misleading data are supplied by the test author and publisher. This serves two functions: it decreases the use of inadequate tests, and emphasizes to the publisher the desirability of following good test practice. Make economics and psychometrics set the same research standards.

Effect of Speed on Item-Test Correlation Coefficients

The practice of doing item analyses with items which have been taken under speed conditions has not been entirely abandoned. Although most careful psychometricians have cautioned against this procedure, several instances have come to the writer's attention recently in which the warnings have been unread or ignored. The reason, perhaps, may be that empirical demonstrations have not been sufficiently publicized to bring the principles to the attention of all of us who should be aware of them. Since the principles can to a large extent be theoretically derived, we have tended to rely on theoretical discussions rather than on the presentation of experimental data. The present paper is intended to offer a discussion of theory and some supporting data.

In the construction of objective tests, one sometimes deliberately injects a factor of speed because of the conviction that speed is an important component of the ability to be measured. More frequently, this is *not* the reason. In most group tests, especially those designed for selection purposes, the speed factor represents a compromise for the sake of administrative efficiency. If it were feasible, untimed power tests would be used in the practical situation; since it is rarely expedient to use untimed tests, time limits are set which are often quite short. In setting these limits, it is assumed that there is considerable correlation between scores on the speeded test and the scores which would result if the test were given under power conditions. This assumption has sometimes been shown to have considerable validity; usually, the assumption is not even investigated.

A decision as to whether speed is an important component of the trait being measured, or whether it is a practical expedient, should be made before test construction is begun. If speed is an essential component, then

From *Educational and Psychological Measurement*, 1949, 9, 51-57. Reprinted by permission.

the criterion used in selecting items should take account of speed. If speed is recognized as an expedient, the criterion should be one which takes into account only power aspects of the ability. In this study the decision was made in advance that measurement of power was the real goal, and that speed was not to be regarded as an essential component. On this basis, the criterion score with which items were to be correlated was a power-test score—one obtained without time limits. It should be noted that a good outside criterion would have been preferred, had it been available. But, as is true of the construction of many tests, it was impractical to obtain such an outside measure and the best available internal criterion was selected.

This study was aimed at investigating the extent to which difficulty values and item-test coefficients obtained under power-test conditions would have changed if the tests had been given under speed conditions. Two experimental forms (A and B) of a general intelligence test were prepared, each containing 138 items. The four types of items in each form were presented in cycle-omnibus fashion in the following order: (1) Analogy, (2) Analogy, (3) Synonym, (4) Classification, (5) Arithmetic computation, (6) Analogy, (7) Analogy, (8) Synonym, (9) Classification, (10) Arithmetic computation, etc. The items were arranged within each item form according to the guessed level of difficulty; how successful this guessed order was may be seen by inspecting the difficulty values in Table I.

The tests were administered to a group of applicants to schools of nursing.[1] One hundred and twenty of these women took Form A and one hundred and twelve took Form B of the test. Their instructions were to work as rapidly as possible and to mark, at successive five-minute signals, the item on which they were working. All applicants were permitted to finish the test; the shortest time taken was between 15 and 20 minutes, the longest time between 30 and 35 minutes. The number of the item each applicant had reached at the end of each five-minute interval was recorded on her test sheet by the scorers.

For purposes of constructing the desired test, item-test correlations against the total score on the test were computed. For purposes of the investigation herein reported, however, a different set of data was gathered. The author arbitrarily hypothesized two tests, each consisting of the first eighty items of the longer experimental forms. He further hypothesized that these eighty-item tests had been given with a ten-minute time limit. He was then able to score each test in terms of the number of items (out of the first eighty) correctly answered in the first ten minutes.

---

[1]The author is indebted to Edith M. Potts, Director, Nurse Testing Division, The Psychological Corporation, for these subjects.

An item analysis performed on this eighty-item, ten-minute test would indicate the results which might be expected if a speed test of the kind hypothesized had actually been administered. Such an analysis was made, using the upper 27 per cent and lower 27 per cent (based on the 138 item power forms) of the applicants taking each form. The proportions of the upper and lower groups passing each item were located on the Flanagan chart devised to provide item-test coefficients for such groups. These values (Speed r_{it}) appear in Table I for Forms A and B.

In obtaining the proportion of applicants passing an item, the fiction of an eighty-item, ten-minute test was maintained. A subject who passed an item *after* the first ten minutes was not included in the passing group; had only ten minutes been available, she would not have reached the item, and therefore would not have passed it. In this way, the conditions of the fictional speeded test were observed.

Since, in fact, we have available the responses of all applicants to all of the eighty items, item-test coefficients can also be computed which will include all applicants who passed an item, regardless of whether it was passed before or after the expiration of ten minutes. Coefficients thus computed may be properly considered power-test coefficients. These coefficients are presented alongside the speed coefficients in Table I.

As we inspect the item-test coefficients, we find that for the first twenty-eight items of Form A, and the first forty-one items of Form B, there is no difference under the speed vs. power conditions. This reflects the fact that all applicants in both the upper and lower groups reached those items in the first ten minutes. As we proceed further into the table, differences begin to appear. These differences indicate that some applicants in the lower groups could have answered the items correctly, had they been able to *reach* those items within ten minutes. As we reach item 70 in each form, the differences in item-test coefficients under speed and power conditions are caused by the failure of applicants in the upper as well as the lower groups to reach items 70 to 80 within the prescribed time limit.

Perhaps the most dramatic aspect of the decreases in item-test r as we turn from speed to power conditions is their unpredictability. Knowing the coefficient under speed conditions, we can make no reasonable guess as to what the power coefficient will be. We can usually be certain that the coefficient will decrease; whether it will still be respectably large after it decreases, or whether its significance will disappear, cannot be foretold.

For example, in Form A, item 56 has a speed item-test coefficient of .77; under power conditions, this value falls to .51, which still leaves the item extremely valuable. Its neighbor, item 57, starts with a speed coefficient of .72, which falls away to exactly .00 under power conditions.

It is obvious that the high item-test coefficient obtained for item 57 under speed conditions is purely an artifact of its late location within the

TABLE I. Average Per Cent Passing and Item-Test Coefficients under Speed and Power Conditions

| | Form A | | | | Form B | | | |
| | SPEED Average* % | | POWER Average* % | | SPEED Average* % | | POWER Average* % | |
Item	Passing	r_{it}	Passing	r_{it}	Passing	r_{it}	Passing	r_{it}
1	87	.30			97	.33		
2	79	.45			96	.40		
3	100	.00			99	.23		
4	97	.33			73	.31		
5	92	.23			96	.14		
6	88	.58			99	.23		
7	97	.33			93	.49		
8	100	.00			100	.00		
9	85	.35			96	.14		
10	85	.62			79	.45		
11	64	.34			68	.46		
12	84	.51			97	.33		
13	97	.00	Same as		100	.00		
14	66	.03	under speed		97	.33		
15	79	.00	conditions.		82	.19		
16	90	.55			73	.15		
17	52	.26			76	.41		
18	96	.40			91	.15	Same as	
19	87	.45			44	.47	under speed	
20	75	.12			78	.71	conditions.	
21	64	.20			97	.33		
22	79	.15			79	.36		
23	90	.55			99	.23		
24	94	.45			88	.13		
25	84	.37			75	.19		
26	70	.28			85	.33		
27	70	.28			75	.04		
28	99	.23			97	.33		
29	81	.43	82	.40	60	.16		
30	94	.45	96	.40	96	.40		
31	90	.55	91	.52	90	.21		
32	91	.52	93	.49	67	.42		
33	84	.51	85	.48	94	.45		
34	93	.09	94	.00	70	.28		
35	78	.38	75	.35	91	.34		
36	90	.55	90	.55	94	.45		
37	67	.27	67	.27	12	.13		
38	94	.22	96	.14	97	.00		
39	88	.26	90	.21	81	.14		
40	84	.51	87	.45	85	.22		
41	88	.58	91	.52	56	.47		

TABLE I. *(Continued)*

	Form A				Form B			
	SPEED		POWER		SPEED		POWER	
Item	Average* % Passing	r_{it}	Average* % Passing	r_{it}	Average* % Passing	r_{it}	Average* % Passing	r_{it}
42	81	.23	84	.15	88	.42	90	.38
43	90	.38	93	.29	99	.23	100	.00
44	91	.52	96	.40	78	−.05	81	−.14
45	82	.10	84	.05	61	.46	64	.40
46	88	.43	94	.23	43	.32	44	.29
47	88	.58	91	.52	46	.38	49	.30
48	78	.71	79	.70	90	.55	96	.40
49	91	.52	100	.00	67	.49	70	.43
50	84	.51	91	.34	79	.45	90	.21
51	76	.41	88	.13	64	.53	73	.38
52	58	.26	63	.16	58	.50	65	.38
53	71	.57	82	.40	62	.68	75	.53
54	62	.37	73	.15	73	.75	99	.23
55	65	.65	84	.37	65	.65	93	.09
56	59	.77	84	.51	68	.79	94	.45
57	67	.72	97	.00	50	.73	64	.53
58	40	.64	58	.26	29	.49	42	.13
59	56	.76	81	.43	64	.82	94	.45
60	58	.80	88	.42	61	.78	90	.38
61	46	.84	65	.51	56	.76	82	.40
62	73	.82	50	.46	55	.89	85	.63
63	53	.80	97	−.33	47	.85	70	.52
64	56	.88	93	.49	56	.88	94	.45
65	47	.75	72	.33	55	.84	90	.38
66	53	.91	93	.49	52	.87	82	.53
67	50	.84	91	.15	47	.85	72	.49
68	50	.90	79	.58	49	.87	79	.45
69	53	.22	55	.20	55	.89	96	.40
70	70	.81	67	.14	82	.86	72	.33
71	79	.84	81	.55	43	.74	72	.40
72	73	.82	81	.46	67	.80	59	.36
73	76	.83	90	.38	82	.86	79	.58
74	67	.80	85	.33	73	.82	68	.46
75	61	.78	84	.26	70	.82	93	.09
76	42	.70	47	.29	67	.80	84	.26
77	52	.74	75	.28	70	.82	97	.33
78	55	.75	96	.40	27	.61	26	.35
79	52	.74	94	.45	52	.74	88	.00
80	30	.63	44	.41	55	.75	100	.00

*These are obtained by averaging the per cents passing in the upper and lower criterion groups.

test. Similarly, its difficulty value under speed conditions is the identical kind of artifact. Had item 57 been made item 1 instead, the average per cent passing it would have been 97 per cent, instead of 67 per cent. The difficulty of an easy item is just as poorly evaluated under speed conditions as the item's internal consistency. A ridiculously easy item, of no true discriminating power, will appear more difficult and highly valid if placed far enough along in the test. Thus, we can predict with considerable confidence, that had item 70 of Form A been "write your own name," the speed item-test coefficient would have been at least .84, and the average per cent passing would have been no higher than 50 per cent.

It is clear, then, that item-test coefficients and item-difficulty indices derived under speed conditions are highly ambiguous. It may be proposed that they might be made more satisfactory if they were based only on subjects who actually responded to each item, thereby removing the effect of "omits." This is not an entirely satisfactory solution. Dr. Davis, in his excellent monograph on item-analysis data, deplores the use of speed tests when item analysis is intended and notes the difficulties which arise when some of the subjects do not reach every item. He recognizes that if tests are speeded there are two alternatives: (1) to include in the item analysis only those who have reached the item, or (2) to include the "non-reads" in the analysis group. He prefers to base the analysis on the group which reaches the item, even though this results in a constantly decreasing number of subjects, in the expressed belief that this is the lesser of the two evils. The writer tends to agree that including those who fail to reach an item in the analysis is the greater evil, but he wonders whether one can really choose between them. When the correlation between speed and power is zero, one might argue that those who reach an item are more or less representative of the entire group. For the tests used in this study, the correlation between the eighty-item speed scores and scores based on those same eighty items under power conditions was about .75. Correlation of that magnitude is strong evidence that those who reach the later items are more proficient and therefore unrepresentative.

The most satisfactory procedure seems to be to give the test in its experimental stages under power conditions, allowing enough time for everyone to reach every item. After item analysis and selection have been done on that basis and the items have been ranked in ascending order of difficulty, appropriate time limits should be set and the test run again for normative purposes. The indices which we would obtain if we analyzed the items after injecting speed would not be the same as those obtained under power conditions, but that fact need not be a source of concern. If the items worked under power conditions, they should also work under speed conditions. The effect of mental set, which doubtless changes as we go from power to speed, will probably be of some importance. Its precise effect is difficult to evaluate. We can be quite certain, however, that the change in mental set will not seriously disturb the relative merits of the individual items and that it will not be of the same order of importance as is the placement of the item under speed conditions.

The writer recognizes that the number of cases in his item analysis groups is very small, and that the item-test coefficients and difficulty indices presented in the table are not very reliable. He believes nonetheless that the data are sufficient to substantiate his main thesis—that item-analysis data from speed tests are practically worthless.

References

Cronbach, L.J. "Response Sets and Test Validity." EDUCATIONAL AND PSYCHO-LOGICAL MEASUREMENT, VI (1946), 475-494.

Davis, F.B. "Item-Analysis Data." *Harvard Education Papers, No. 2.* Cambridge: Harvard University Press.

Flanagan, J.C. "General Considerations in the Selection of Test Items and a Short Method of Estimating the Product-Moment Coefficient from the Data at the Tails of the Distribution." *Journal of Educational Psychology,* XXX (1939), 674-680.

Expectancy Tables — A Way of Interpreting Test Validity

"What does a correlation coefficient of .50 mean?" "How can I best interpret to the teachers in my school the meaning of validity coefficients?" "How can I demonstrate to my boss that the tests we are using are successful, when he doesn't understand statistical terminology?" These questions inevitably come up in the experience of any serious test user or consultant. Statistically adequate replies are not sufficient (nor are they often appropriate) to meet the problems posed by these queries. A device is needed which can simply and directly reveal the relationships between test scores and performance measures to those who lack the necessary background to understand even the more commonplace statistical terms such as correlation, standard deviation, and variance.

It is easy to sit back in one's chair and insist that anyone who works with tests should have a thorough grounding in basic statistics. This is a laudable philosophy – one can only agree, "Yes, it would be nice." As a matter of practical fact, the success or failure of many test programs depends on our ability to communicate understanding of test results to colleagues who are statistically untrained – to teachers who will use the results in their classrooms or vote for the continuation or rejection of programs in the schools; to superiors in industry who will or will not budget funds for personnel selection through tests; to labor union representatives who question the use of tests by management. These people cannot be sent to the university for a statistics course. They must be informed of the meaning of test results in *their* language, not the language of the technician.

This article deals with a device which can do much to meet this need – the expectancy table.

The expectancy table is not new; it has been known and used in the test field for more than a quarter of a century. But it has not been as widely

From *Test Service Bulletin* No. 38, The Psychological Corporation, 1949.

known or used as it deserves. In the course of developing newer and more complex statistical techniques for the construction and analysis of tests and test batteries, we have too far neglected the communication of understanding to the less initiated. It is to be hoped that this neglect will be recognized and remedied.

An expectancy table is merely a grid (see Figure 1) containing a number of cells. Along the side are indicated the test score intervals; along the top are placed the course grades which have been awarded, the production record or supervisor's rating, the scores on an end-of-term achievement test, or whatever other criterion of success is desired. For each individual we place a tally which shows, vertically, his test score and, horizontally, his rank on the criterion. (Thus, in Figure 1, a student scoring 62 on the Sentences section of the *DAT Language Usage* test and earning a B in

FIGURE 1. Expectancy grid showing how students' grades in Rhetoric and previously-earned scores on the *DAT Sentences Test* are tallied in appropriate cells. (Data from Kansas State Teachers College; grade of F = failure, no grade of E given; N = 100 freshman girls; mean test score = 48.58, S.D. = 15.2, r = .71)

Scores on DAT Sentences Test	Grades in Rhetoric					Totals
	F	D	C	B	A	
80-89					/ ⁽¹⁾	1
70-79				/ ⁽¹⁾	//// ⁽⁴⁾	5
60-69			/// ⁽³⁾	HHt HHt //// ⁽¹⁴⁾	HHt ⁽⁵⁾	22
50-59			HHt //// ⁽⁹⁾	HHt /// ⁽⁸⁾	HHt / ⁽⁶⁾	23
40-49		/// ⁽³⁾	HHt HHt /// ⁽¹³⁾	HHt / ⁽⁶⁾		22
30-39	/ ⁽¹⁾	/// ⁽³⁾	HHt //// ⁽⁹⁾	/// ⁽³⁾		16
20-29	/ ⁽¹⁾	//// ⁽⁴⁾	/// ⁽³⁾			8
10-19		// ⁽²⁾				2
0-9		/ ⁽¹⁾				1
	2	13	37	32	16	100

Rhetoric would be plotted in the bold-outlined cell.) When the tallying has been completed, the tallies in each cell are added, and this number is recorded in the cell. The numbers in each row of cells are then added and the sum is recorded at the right of each row; the numbers in each column are added and the sum is recorded at the bottom of each column.[1] We now have our basic data for an expectancy table, which may be organized in several ways depending on our primary interest.

I. Suppose that we wish to answer the question, "What is the probability that a student with a given test score will succeed in a specified course?" Table I presents the data organized to answer this question.

TABLE I. Expectancy table prepared from the grid in Figure 1. The left-hand table summarizes the frequencies as they appear in the original grid. The right-hand table shows these frequencies converted into per cents.

Total No.	Number receiving each grade					Test Scores	Per cent receiving each grade					Total Per cent
	F	D	C	B	A		F	D	C	B	A	
1					1	80–89					100	100
5				1	4	70–79				20	80	100
22			3	14	5	60–69			14	63	23	100
23			9	8	6	50–59			39	35	26	100
22		3	13	6		40–49		14	59	27		100
16	1	3	9	3		30–39	6	19	56	19		100
8	1	4	3			20–29	13	50	37			100
2		2				10–19		100				100
1		1				0–9		100				100
100	2	13	37	32	16							

Each cell frequency has been converted to a per cent based on the total number of tallies in its row. The table then reads: of the 22 freshman girls who took a course in Rhetoric and had scored between 60 and 69 on the Sentences test, 23% (5 girls) earned a grade of A, 63% (14 girls) earned a B, and 14% (3 girls) earned a C. Not one of the girls whose score was in this group received a grade lower than C in Rhetoric. One might predict then that girls who take this course in future terms, and who have attained scores of 60 to 69 on the *DAT* Sentences test, will probably be better than average students, since all but 14% earned grades of A and B. Interpretations may be made in the same way for other test scores and individuals.

---

[1] If a check on the accuracy of the additions is desired, the sums in the right hand margin may be added, and the numbers at the bottom of the columns may be added. These two totals should be equal to each other, and should also equal the original number of cases we started to plot.

II. Suppose that the question is posed from a different standpoint. "How can we pick out our best applicants?" Starting with a grid just as we did before, but computing the percentages by columns rather than rows, we prepare our expectancy table to answer this question directly. Table II

TABLE II. Expectancy table showing the number and per cent of stenographers of various rated abilities who came from specified score groups on the *S-B Stenographic Proficiency Test*. (N = 52, mean score = 15.4, S.D. = 2.9, r = .61; score is average per letter for five letters)

Number in each score group receiving each rating on stenographic ability				Stenographic Proficiency Test Scores	Per cent in each score group receiving each rating on stenographic ability			
Below Average	Average	Above Average	Excellent		Below Average	Average	Above Average	Excellent
	4	6	7	18–19		17	40	64
	2	2	4	16–17		9	13	36
	10	5		14–15		44	33	
	4	1		12–13		17	7	
2	2	1		10–11	67	9	7	
1	1			8–9	33	4		
3	23	15	11		100	100	100	100

shows such a table for 52 employed stenographers who took the *Seashore-Bennett Stenographic Proficiency Test*. Their test scores are shown at the left, their ratings on stenographic ability at the top. The righthand column then reads: of the eleven stenographers rated excellent, 64% (7 girls) scored 18-19 on the test and the remaining 36% (4 girls) scored 16-17. None of the girls rated excellent scored below 16 on the *Stenographic Proficiency Test*. We can therefore expect our future excellent stenographers to come from those scoring 16 and higher on the test. Note that the expectancy table does *not* predict that all those who achieve scores of 16 or better will prove excellent. Some of them may be those rated above average or only average. It predicts that most of those who will later prove excellent will probably have come out of this high-scoring group.

III. A similar approach, primarily diagrammatic in form, may be used to answer the question, "What is the probability that an office worker will attain an average rating or higher?" Again starting from a basic grid such as is shown in Figure 1, we prepare a graph which is focused entirely at the single category: average and above. For each score group, we calculate the per cent of that group which has received ratings of average or better. The data in Table III are based on 65 office workers who had previously taken the *General Clerical Test*. The material in Table III is read as follows: of the 11 office workers who scored between 50 and 99 on the *General*

TABLE III. Expectancy table and graph showing per cent expected to rate average or better in office clerical tasks on the basis of scores on the *General Clerical Test*. (N = 65, mean score = 136.1, S.D. = 39.1, r_{bis} = .31)

General Clerical Test Scores	No. in score group	No. rated average or better	% rated average or better						
200–up	5	5	100						
150–199	18	15	83						
100–149	31	23	74						
50–99	11	6	55						
Total	65			0%	20%	40%	60%	80%	100%

Clerical Test, 6 of them (55%) later received supervisory ratings of average or better; of the 31 workers who scored between 100 and 149 on this test, 23 (74%) earned ratings of average or better than average, etc. A glance at the diagram indicates the chances that an applicant with a given score will earn a satisfactory rating as an office worker in this company. One who scores over 200 on the test is almost twice as likely to be satisfactory as one who scores below 100.

The *advantages* of the expectancy table will be self-evident to those who have the problem of interpreting test predictions to teachers and parents, business superiors, and applicants for employment. As is true of most aids, there are *limitations* of which the user of expectancy tables should be aware. Some of these, together with questions which have been asked concerning such tables, are noted below.

Q. Is there any set number of test score groups, or criterion categories, which is most desirable?

A. No. Expectancy tables may consist of as few as four cells (two score groups along the left-hand margin, and two criterion ratings – e.g., pass vs. fail – along the top), or as many as the data will permit. The optimum number is that which best serves the purpose – which best summarizes the relationship we wish to illustrate. The tables used above as illustrations have deliberately been prepared with different numbers of cells, score groups, and criterion categories. Each of the tables might equally well have been prepared in some other way. One guiding principle is to make the number of cells proportional to the number of individuals; the fewer the individuals, the fewer the number of cells.

Q. How does the expectancy table differ from a scatter diagram used for computation of a correlation coefficient?

A. The basic data appearing on the grid from which the expectancy table is prepared are the same as those in a scatter diagram. In fact, a correlation chart can be used to plot these data. The chief difference is in the handling of the data. The expectancy table organizes the material for interpretation of an *individual's chances of success.* The validity coefficient summarizes such data for an *entire group* in one mathematical figure. The expectancy table makes apparent the details of the data at various parts of the distributions; the coefficient, being a kind of average, obscures those details just as any averaging does.

Q. How much confidence may we place in the predictions made on the basis of expectancy tables?

A. The reliability of any statistical measure varies directly with the number of individuals on which the measure is based. Since each cell is likely to contain relatively few cases, the confidence to which we are entitled is less than for measures based on larger numbers of cases. One should recall that the average score of a class is a more stable figure than the score of any individual student. The lesser reliability of individual cell entries (or per cents) is a real limitation of the expectancy table technique, and one of which the user should always be conscious. The limitation is not so great as to vitiate the usefulness of the device. The coefficients computed in most school and industrial situations also fall short of ideal levels of reliability. The lesser reliability of the figures in any expectancy table is frequently compensated for by the clearer interpretation they permit. It should also be remarked that larger frequencies in each cell, and consequently greater permissible confidence in our predictions, may be obtained by lumping together adjacent score groups or criterion ratings. For example, if in Table II our score intervals had been plotted as 8-13 and 14-19, and our ratings as average and below vs. above average and excellent, the result would be Table IV, in which the cells have greater frequencies than do those of Table II. Of course, this also obscures some of the relationships. The user will have to decide which is more important in a given situation.

Q. Can expectancy charts be inferred directly from correlation coefficients?

A. This suggestion is more likely to come from colleagues who are mainly teachers of counselors and personnel men than from those who are actually on the "firing line" and have to deal with real classes and employees. Theoretically, knowing a correlation coefficient one can prepare the scatter diagram (and therefore the expectancy table) which

TABLE IV. Expectancy table reducing the number of cells in Table II from twenty-four to four.

Average and Below Average	Excellent and Above Average	*Stenographic Proficiency Test Scores*	Average and Below Average	Excellent and Above Average
16	24	14–19	62%	92%
10	2	8–13	38%	8%
26	26		100%	100%

it summarizes.[2] A practical difficulty is that one can do so only when a large number of cases is involved – far larger than one ordinarily finds in a school and industrial situation. With the smaller numbers of cases usually available (50, 100, 150 or even 200), irregularities in the distributions do not permit such inference. Two quite different irregular scatter diagrams may result in the same validity coefficient.

Many users of expectancy tables *will* wish to combine the virtues of such tables with those of validity coefficients by using the same scatter diagram as a basis for both approaches. This tactic is, of course, eminently acceptable.

Q. Do we have to compute per cents for each cell in the expectancy tables, or can we see relationships without doing so?

A. The computation of per cents is useful primarily as a way of rendering the figures in each row or column comparable. If we wish to say that John's chances of making good in a course or on a job are 73 out of 100, while Fred's chances are only 33 out of 100, the computation of per cents is necessary. If we are satisfied with knowing that a person's chances are 10 out of 13, or are 23 to 7 in his favor, the frequencies alone may be entirely adequate. Whether frequencies or per cents are used is a matter of individual preference and individual success in communicating the meaning of the data to others.

Q. Is the expectancy table susceptible to other uses than predicting chances of success?

A. One of the most valuable uses of an expectancy table (and of a scatter diagram) is that it helps identify the individuals for whom our predic-

---

[2]Actually, a number of such theoretical charts have been prepared showing expectancy tables which are derived from specified coefficients. One such collection is that of Jackson, R. W. B. and Phillips, A. J. Prediction Efficiencies by Deciles for Various Degrees of Relationship. *Educational Research Series* No. 11, Dept. of Educ. Research, Ontario College of Education, University of Toronto.

tions of success have gone astray, or those who do not conform to the usual ability patterns. By investigating the personal characteristics and backgrounds of such deviate individuals, we often find clues to unrecognized factors predictive of success or failure in a course or job. For example, by noting over several years those freshmen whose academic performances were much better, or much worse, than was predicted from their scores, one college dean was able to identify several facts which would modify his future predictions – e.g., boys from high school X had particularly good study habits, those from school Y were unusually test-wise, etc. By pointing out instances in which prediction missed, the expectancy table permitted going back to the individual – always a healthy step in appraisal of people or programs.

In short, the expectancy table is a tool, and one of potentially considerable value. Like any tool, its usefulness depends on the extent to which it is understood and on the ingenuity and skill of its user. Properly understood, it represents an excellent medium for interpretation and communication of the meaning of test results.

Separation of Sex Groups
in Test Reporting

The literature on sex differences in learning has long ago demonstrated that boys and girls acquire knowledge and skills selectively. One need not attribute these differences to biological predispositions, since our culture provides differential experience to the two sexes, and consequently differential opportunity and motivation for learning in specific areas. The present paper deals not with the theory of sex differences, but with the need for recognizing them in test construction, standardization and interpretation.

Most well-conceived research in the intelligence testing field has revealed little or no difference between the sexes. This may be a reflection of true equality between girls and boys. It is equally attributable to the way in which the tests have been constructed. In the 1937 revision of the Stanford-Binet, for example, the individual tasks were so selected as to result in equality of performance by the two sexes. Those tasks which resulted in an imbalance favoring one sex or the other were eliminated. The wholly defensible assumption was made that "test batteries of extensive scope and varied content as a rule yield only small sex differences in total scores, and that when individual test items do show large sex differences these can often be accounted for in terms of known differences in environment and training."[1] In this case, it is recognized that the assumption of native equality in ability is being made, and the tasks are deliberately chosen to fulfill that assumption. This is not the same as combining total scores into a single distribution without prior selection and investigation of the items with respect to sex differences. It is not sufficient

[1]McNemar, Quinn, *The Revision of The Stanford-Binet Scale*, An Analysis of the Standardization Data, Houghton Mifflin Company, 1942, p. 43.

justification for other constructors of intelligence tests to make the tacit assumption of equality between sexes without investigating sex differences on either the individual items or on total score. If real differences on total score do appear, there is an obligation to report separate sex distributions.

Achievement test results have for many years demonstrated selective superiority of boys and girls. Boys are generally superior in arithmetic, science and history; girls usually excel in reading, languages and the arts. Yet, although this is common knowledge, achievement tests in these and other subjects rarely present sex-differentiated norms. Even the best-standardized tests, such as the Stanford and Metropolitan batteries, are accompanied by combined norms. Data from the recent standardization of the Metropolitan Achievement Tests have been made available to the writer.[2] These data show that seventh-grade girls score as well on the English tests as eighth-grade boys. On the other hand, eighth-grade girls score little better on the History and Civics test, and no better on the Geography test than seventh-grade boys.

Where such sex differences exist, two kinds of justification might be advanced for ignoring them. It might be proposed that the norms are intended to indicate how much of a given subject-matter students should have learned at specified age and grade levels, and the goals should be the same for boys and girls. If this is the operating principle, then norms should not be derived statistically at all. Norms as goals should be decided by educational philosophers and administrators without reference to test score distributions. Since manuals stress that their norms are descriptions of what exists, rather than what should be, this argument must be rejected.

The second approach to justifying combined sex norms is that a given student competes with boys and girls in his studies, and should therefore be compared with both. The principle of comparing a student with his competition must be accepted as valid; but is that competition primarily with the combined sex group? Boys and girls differ considerably in their ability to spell. Spelling is the best predictor uncovered thus far of success in stenography. The proportion of boys in any stenography class is ordinarily very small indeed. Similarly, some girls may choose mechanical curricula, but they will be few and far between. And those who do will find their competition almost entirely male. Additional examples of single sex specialization could be added in large numbers: from educational spheres when students go to non-co-educational institutions as well as professional and vocational areas where one or the other sex is largely predominant.

Achievement tests are used for prediction of vocational success, but aptitude tests are even more widely used for this purpose. The data presented in Table I were prepared from distributions of scores on the

---

[2]The writer is indebted to World Book Co., publishers of the Metropolitan Achievement Tests, for these data.

TABLE I. Score Equivalents of Designated Percentiles for Boys and Girls Separately and Combined — Tenth Grade

Differential Aptitude Tests — Form A

Percentile	Verbal Score			Num. Score			Abs. Score			Space Score			Mech. Reas. Score			Cler. Score			Spell. Score			Sent. Score			Percentile
	B	G	T	B	G	T	B	G	T	B	G	T	B	G	T	B	G	T	B	G	T	B	G	T	
95	39	39	39	33	31	33	42	41	41	83	73	79	57	41	54	71	83	80	85	90	88	57	64	63	95
90	35	35	35	30	29	30	39	39	39	76	67	73	54	37	50	65	75	73	78	86	84	51	59	57	90
80	31	30	31	27	24	26	36	35	35	69	57	64	50	32	44	60	69	65	66	78	74	44	53	49	80
75	30	29	29	25	23	24	35	33	34	65	53	60	48	31	41	58	67	63	62	75	71	42	50	46	75
70	28	27	28	24	22	23	34	32	33	63	49	57	46	29	39	56	65	61	56	72	67	40	47	44	70
60	25	24	25	21	19	20	31	29	30	56	41	48	43	26	34	53	62	58	49	66	60	36	43	40	60
50	23	22	22	18	17	18	29	26	28	47	35	40	40	23	30	51	59	55	41	60	52	32	39	36	50
40	20	19	19	16	15	15	26	23	25	37	28	32	37	20	26	49	56	53	34	52	44	28	36	32	40
30	17	16	17	14	13	13	23	19	21	26	22	24	33	17	23	46	53	50	25	45	35	23	30	27	30
25	16	15	16	12	11	12	21	16	19	22	19	20	31	16	20	45	52	48	21	40	30	21	28	25	25
20	14	14	14	11	10	11	19	13	16	18	15	17	28	14	18	43	50	46	16	36	24	18	25	22	20
10	11	11	11	7	7	7	9	4	7	10	10	10	21	10	13	38	45	42	5	20	11	11	19	15	10
5	8	8	8	4	4	4	2	1	1	4	5	5	15	5	8	34	40	37	2	7	3	3	12	8	5

Differential Aptitude Tests, a series including tests of Verbal Reasoning, Numerical Ability, Abstract Reasoning, Space Relations, Mechanical Reasoning, Clerical Speed and Accuracy, Spelling and Sentences. The Interpretive Manual of the Differential Aptitude Tests presents norms separately for boys and girls for each grade from VIII through XII. For purposes of this study, one grade only—the tenth—was selected as a demonstration of the effect of ignoring sex differences.

Boys' and girls' scores on each of the eight tests were thrown together into single combined distributions, and the scores which fell at designated percentile points were found. These scores were then compared with the scores and percentile equivalents which appear in the Manual. These are the data which are shown in Table I. The table is read as follows: to obtain a percentile rank of 50 on the boys' norms of the Verbal Reasoning Test, a tenth-grade boy would need a score of 23; a girl would need a score of 22 to reach the 50th percentile on girls' norms; and either of them would need a score of 22 to reach the 50th percentile on norms based on a combined distribution.

The Verbal and Numerical percentile equivalents do not indicate the presence of sex differences on these tests. On the Abstract Reasoning Test, there are small differences in favor of the boys; but, if only the combined distribution were used for counseling, the judgments would not vary from those based on single sex scores. A boy whose score of 34 placed him at the 70th percentile on the boys' distribution would be found at the 75th percentile on the combined scale.

The Space Relations Test, however, begins to show more sizable sex differences. The percentile equivalent differs by about ten points, depending on whether the single sex or combined distribution is used. A boy whose score of 56 placed him at the 60th percentile for boys would be at about the 70th percentile on the combined distribution. The most dramatic differences favoring the boys appear on the Mechanical Reasoning Test. Counseling would be very different if one had only the combined distribution available rather than the ones based on single sex scores. For example, a boy with a Mechanical Reasoning score of 40 would be close to the 75th percentile on a combined distribution scale. With only that information, the counselor would be impelled to consider him as having enough ability to compete favorably in a curriculum or occupation requiring mechanical understanding. If he entered such a curriculum or occupation, however, his competition would be almost entirely male. Compared with boys only, his score of 40 leaves him at the 50th percentile, a ranking not at all superior.

The differences on the Clerical, Spelling and Sentences tests all definitely favor the girls. A girl scoring 53 on the Clerical Test would be at the 40th percentile on a combined distribution, but at only the 30th percentile on a girls' scale. If she scored 52 on the Spelling Test she would be at the 50th percentile on a combined scale, and the 40th percentile of a girls' distribution. A girl's score of 36 on the Sentences Test is at the 50th percentile on a combined distribution, and at the 40th percentile of a girls' scale.

It is clear from these data that to the extent that competition in any curriculum or vocation comes preponderantly from a single sex, separate sex norms are needed for test score interpretation. Thus, a girl who intends entering a mechanical field should be considered against boys' norms. If her chances of success are to be promising, her score must be extremely good for her sex; if she is to equal the 75th percentile for boys, she must be at the 99th percentile for girls.

With respect to reliability, the writer has not seen fit to make as complete an analysis as has been made for the discussion of norms. Table III of the Differential Aptitude Test Manual presents reliability coefficients for each sex for each grade from the eighth through the twelfth inclusive. This table shows sex differences in test reliability in most instances, but not many of these differences are practically important; in fact, on the same test the higher coefficient may be found for boys in one grade and for girls in another grade. Some important differences do appear, however. On the Clerical Test in the eighth grade both Forms A and B show a difference of .10 in reliability (.77 boys and .87 girls). In Mechanical Reasoning, the reliability coefficients for boys are consistently higher (by .12 to .17) than for girls. The stability of scores on these tests must be evaluated quite differently for the two sexes.

That validity coefficients will show sex differences follows naturally from the previous considerations. Since the reliability of a test acts as a ceiling on validity, sex variation in reliability must be reflected in validity variation. Furthermore, it has been noted that boys and girls frequently enter different curricula and occupations. Since there is no such thing as 'the' validity of a test — since validity is specific to the criterion — the very fact of differences in choice of courses and jobs makes separate validity coefficients mandatory. A third consideration may be that boys and girls use different abilities to achieve success. As one example of sex differences in validity, we may cite the following coefficients between twelfth-grade English marks and Differential Aptitude Test scores in a Hamilton, Ohio, high school:

	Differential Aptitude Test	
	Boys (N = 119)	Girls (N = 146)
Verbal	.61	.58
Numerical	.49	.59
Abstract	.32	.46
Space	.22	.33
Mechanical	.06	.38
Clerical	.14	.20
Spelling	.60	.40
Sentences	.66	.69

Several explanations of these differences might be proposed. The point being made here is simply that the differences do exist, and warrant reporting.

It might well be suggested that if we agree to the desirability of having separate sex norms, we ought also to agree to separate vocational goal norms, separate curricular norms, separate city norms — in fact, separate norms for every conceivable kind of group with which those who take tests are likely to compete. This sounds like an ambitious undertaking — probably too ambitious to be practically possible. The writer agrees that it is perhaps over-ambitious. He, nevertheless, affirms that considerable progress toward the goal is possible; that progress toward the goal is highly desirable; and that, by wise selection of the most important areas needing differential reporting, we can promptly and notably increase the usefulness of tests for selection and guidance purposes alike.

Verbal Factors

I am afraid that I do not know what *the* Verbal Factor is. When I worked with the Graduate Record Examination, we leased three verbal tests from the College Entrance Examination Board — a vocabulary-opposites test, a double-definitions test, and a paragraph-meaning test — and called the total score from these three our Verbal Factor. Thurstone has proposed V (Verbal Relations) as a verbal factor, but he also recognizes his W (or Word Fluency) factor as being verbal in nature. In the Differential Aptitude Tests we have a Verbal Reasoning Test, but we have a Language Usage Test, composed of Spelling and Sentences, which also contributes to measurement of verbal ability. Further, if the factor analysis research on Mechanical Comprehension in the Air Corps, as reported by Guilford, can be generalized to our Mechanical Reasoning Test, then the MR test, too, has some saturation in the Verbal Factor as it is defined there.

Perhaps the foregoing is evidence only of the impurity or factorial complexity of the several tests. An alternative explanation which seems to warrant consideration is that perhaps *the* Verbal Factor is not yet sufficiently defined or understood. It may well be that the course of wisdom is to recognize the possibility that there is not one Verbal Factor but several Verbal Factors. There is increasing evidence that memory, which was regarded as a unitary factor for some time, must be recognized as several factors. It seems equally possible that continued research will demonstrate that there are several Verbal Factors as well. There is strong suspicion in the minds of many of us that in discussing the Verbal Factor we are reifying a mathematical concept, that in trying to make mathematically derived factors psychologically meaningful we have sometimes acted as though our labels gave them psychological existence and character. I, for one, am not at all certain that the Verbal Factor as derived from different sets of tests and different populations is psychologically invariant.

Neither am I certain that the factors which result from analysis of test results alone are the best measures of the ability or abilities with which we may be concerned in aptitude studies. I have in mind some results reported in the same Air Corps volume to which I previously referred. In that volume reasons were discussed as to why the Verbal Factor was necessary for pilots, bombardiers, and navigators. We are then informed that their vocabulary test is "practically a pure measure of the Verbal Factor" and that "in a battery where measurement of the Verbal Factor is required, a vocabulary test is strongly to be recommended."

As we continue, however, we learn of a startling development:

> Owing to its limited predictive value, the Vocabulary Test was dropped from the classification battery in the summer of 1942. It was replaced by the Technical Vocabulary Test, which is a test of specific technical information pertaining to piloting, navigation, and bombardiering. This test, although related to vocabulary, and loaded with the Verbal Factor (0.41 for the pilot score), possessed a validity of .21 for pilots. Part of this validity is derived from the test's loading with the mechanical experience factor (0.39). The remaining part is accounted for by its loading with pilot interest (0.34).

It appears then that when this pure measure of the Verbal Factor was exposed to validation against a criterion, it lost much of its luster. Yet it is the very process of validation against an outside criterion which must be the final yardstick in determining the value of the Verbal Factor or any other factor in aptitude testing. We have heard much in the last few years about factorial validity. This may be a useful concept for theoretical research purposes; it is not a substitute for empirical validation. Tests constructed in the light of factorial research must be subjected to empirical validation just as much as tests built according to different principles.

It is my belief, then, that the external criterion must determine the nature of the Verbal Factor as used in aptitude test batteries. If the criterion is one which calls for ability to read and understand technical writing, a test of that ability may be the best measure of Verbal Factor for that criterion. If a knowledge of words and their meaning is important, a general vocabulary or technical vocabulary test may be best. If the ability to reason with verbal constructs is required by the criterion, a verbal reasoning test may provide the greatest situational validity. All of these tests may reasonably be considered as measures of the Verbal Factors.

The problem which faces the aptitude-test constructor is that of preparing a test or group of tests which will predict best in most applications. He may approach his task through factor analysis, or job analysis, or both. He should be swayed by efficiency, face validity, and similar practical considerations; but these are of secondary importance. The prime consideration is still that of building a test which will provide most empirical validity in the greatest number of situations — which will best predict the largest number of criteria. For it is the criterion which, in the last analysis, will define the worth of the factor or the test.

The Three-Legged Coefficient

How low can a correlation coefficient be and still provide useful information? Suppose a test correlates with school grades only to the extent of .25, what shall we do? All too often, the action taken is to throw the test out with no further thought, and to look for some other test in the fond hope that it will do better. If the second test does not correlate appreciably higher, it is in turn discarded and the search for still another test begins. How intelligent is this process? Not very!

A correlation coefficient is not a judgment — it is only a number summarizing the relationship of two sets of facts to each other. It is not a substitute for thinking — quite the contrary, it should be the impulse which starts the thinking process going. The size of a given coefficient is important, but *why* it is that size is much more important. The statistician who evaluates the correlation coefficient in terms of an index of efficiency, a coefficient of alienation, or the percentage of criterion variance accounted for, is performing a useful task. But the more basic, more meaningful step — which must be taken by the counselor, the teacher, the administrator, the personnel man — is to look at the coefficient as a clue to further investigation. This investigation should include not only the *test*, but also the *criterion* (grades or ratings or whatever), the *population* (the particular group of students or employees or patients involved) and any other factors which might have influenced the state of affairs which the coefficient describes.

The following examples will serve to illustrate some situations in which a stereotyped reaction to a coefficient of correlation is unprofitable.

I. A numerical ability test was given to a group of ninth grade boys at the beginning of a school year. It was the intent of the school to use the test as a predictor of success in geometry — i.e., as a geometry aptitude test. At the end of the year, therefore, the guidance director computed the

From *Test Service Bulletin* No. 40, The Psychological Corporation, 1950.

correlation of the students' numerical ability scores with their geometry grades for the year. The coefficient found was about .30—a not very encouraging result. Had the guidance director been less wise, he might well have abandoned the test in favor of another. Instead, he looked up the students' scores on a statewide examination in geometry, and correlated these scores with the numerical ability test scores. The coefficient in this case was over .60—relatively good prediction. The guidance director used the discrepancy between these two correlation coefficients to initiate discussions with the mathematics teachers as to the bases on which grades were being assigned. The teachers agreed to rate competence and work habits separately; the test is being retained as a selection device by the school. Incidentally, both the school administration and parents are finding math grades more useful than before.

II. A personnel manager in a large industrial firm was anxious to install a test of stenographic proficiency to select stenographers and secretaries. As a first step, he gave the test, which involved dictation and transcription at high speed, to all stenographers and secretaries already employed by the organization. He also obtained ratings as to the ability of these employees, and these ratings he correlated with the scores on the proficiency test. To his consternation, the coefficient was quite low. Since the test seemed obviously to be measuring stenographic ability, he began to investigate the ratings.

First he obtained separate coefficients for those called stenographers (who were part of a pool under a stenographic supervisor) and for those called secretaries (each responsible to one or two executives). The correlation of the proficiency test with the stenographic supervisor's ratings was rewardingly good; for secretaries, it was a little worse than it had been originally. The personnel manager discreetly inquired concerning the bases on which the executives rated their secretaries. He was not entirely surprised to find that such factors as assisting in executive decisions, doing personal shopping for the executive, keeping appointments straight, protecting the executive from undesirable visitors, and so on, were (among other factors) affecting the ratings. Though the secretaries might previously have been excellent stenographers, they had lost much of their earlier skill through lack of practice. Consequently, they scored comparatively low on the test, and were rated high by their bosses: the validity coefficient suffered. The personnel manager proceeded to install the test as a selection device for newcomers, with confidence that it would predict well where it needed to — at the stenographer level.

III. In a city which has five high schools, a series of aptitude tests was given to all tenth grade students. Verbal reasoning test scores were correlated with physics grades for all students in the five high schools who had taken that course. The correlation coefficient was quite low, between .15 and .20. The naive approach would have been to disregard the test's usefulness from then on. The research director, however, took steps to find out why the coefficients were no higher — whether the test, or the grades, or some peculiarity of the group of students was responsible. Among other things, he computed separate validity coefficients for each of the five schools and was promptly rewarded: the five coefficients ranged between .30 and .50. It soon became clear why this result might have been expected. The five schools varied considerably in the quality of their pupils, as had previously been demonstrated by intelligence and achievement tests. However, each school gave grades to its students according to their performance as compared with their own classmates. Thus, a performance worth A or B in the poorest school was no better than the performance for which a grade of C or D was assigned in the best school. Under the circumstances, it was inevitable that a low validity coefficient would result when the data from all five schools were combined. Analysis for each school separately revealed the real value of the test.

This same research director demonstrated his understanding of the meaning of test results in interpreting the range of the above coefficients to the teacher-counselors in his schools. The counselor in the school for which the coefficient was only .30 inquired as to why validity was lowest in that school. The director pointed out that that school was the one which drew the best students, and had very few low-ability students. The consequence of this small spread in ability was to make discrimination among the students more difficult. Small spread of scores is always associated with smaller correlation coefficients[1] — the wider the spread in ability, the easier it is to distinguish between the better and poorer performances. Any of us can tell the difference between a midget and a giant at a glance. More precise measurement is needed to distinguish between a man six feet tall and one who is five feet, eleven-and-a-half inches in height. Additional difficult test material would be needed to make discriminations among the superior students as successfully as the present test discriminated among students in general.

IV. A test in American history was used by an eleventh grade teacher at the recommendation of the supervisor of secondary education. The test correlated poorly with the teacher's grades, and the teacher complained to the supervisor that the test was inappropriate for that school. The supervisor persisted in her earlier judgment of the test's worth; she sat down with the history teacher and they analyzed the test items as to whether they were testing for memory of facts or whether they were measuring more complex thought processes. They then rescored the test papers getting one score for "fact" questions and a separate score for "thought" questions. When the teacher's grades were correlated with these new scores, they found that the correlation with the thought part of the test did not improve, while the teacher's grades correlated much better with the scores on fact questions.

---

[1] A formula showing the relation between spread of scores and size of correlation coefficients may be found in many statistical texts.

As a result of this analysis, the history teacher was led to re-examine the way in which grades in the course were being awarded. He realized that, in his own quizzes and mid-term and final examinations, too much stress had been laid on simple memory for facts and too little on ability to use the facts in thinking. Thus the low correlation coefficient between the published test and the teacher's grades led to an important and profitable investigation of his grading system.

V. An eighth grade shop class took tests of mechanical reasoning and space relations at the beginning of the year. At the end of the first term, the scores on these tests were correlated with the teacher's grades. The coefficients were .26 and .13 respectively. When the teacher remarked to the counselor that the tests were apparently useless, the counselor suggested that they suspend judgment until the end of the year. When the second term's grades were in, correlation coefficients were again computed. The mechanical reasoning test correlated .41; the space relations test, .33. In an effort to understand these discrepancies, the counselor asked the shop teacher to describe the tasks the students were assigned. They discovered that the first term's work was almost entirely manipulative, the students having been given explicit instructions concerning every detail of simple projects. During the second term, on the other hand, they were expected to carry forward more complicated assignments with considerably less supervision. They had to imagine what their individual projects would be as finished products and plan how to accomplish the task. A good deal of headwork as well as handwork thus contributed to the quality of the result.

Having recognized these differences in course requirements of the first and second terms, both the shop teacher and the counselor could readily understand why the tests showed up better in one term than in the other. The prediction of second term grades was a more reasonable demand on the tests.

The moral of these illustrations can be stated simply: statistics are not a substitute for thinking. A rating or a grade represents a judgment; a test score is a statement of accomplishment on a specified set of tasks. Regardless of how high or how low a coefficient of correlation may be, these things always demand consideration:

1—how the judgments were arrived at;

2—the nature of the test tasks and their appropriateness in relation to the job or the course; and

3—the peculiarities of the particular group of individuals being studied.

The correlation coefficient has been likened to a three-legged stool: one leg is the predictor (frequently a test), another is the criterion (grades, ratings, etc.) and the third is the population on which the coefficient is obtained (grade level or job family, sex, spread of ability, etc.). He who uses a three-legged stool without ascertaining that all three legs warrant confidence is very likely to be floored.

The Differential Aptitude Tests —
A Five-Year Report

In 1947, the Differential Aptitude Tests were launched in the hope that they might make a significant contribution to the armory of the guidance profession. Now, approximately five years and 4,000 validity coefficients later, it may be well to summarize the experience with these tests. The test scores have been correlated with all kinds of grades in school systems throughout the country; they have been correlated with achievement test scores, interest inventory results, and conventional intelligence tests. Students who took the tests have been retested after three years, have been followed through three-and-a-half subsequent years of high school and have been followed into post-high school educational and vocational careers. What has been learned from this extensive use and research?

In the first place, one may generalize that course grades are usually best predicted by those tests which an experienced counselor would expect to be the best predictors. Thus, the Sentences and Verbal tests are the best predictors of grades in English, the Numerical test is most effective in predicting mathematics and bookkeeping grades, social studies have useful predictors in the Verbal, Sentences, and Numerical tests, and science is best predicted by those same three tests, with Abstract Reasoning also useful. Shorthand is virtually always best predicted by the Spelling test; the Space Relations test is effective for mechanical drawing and plane geometry. The Numerical Ability test has been found to predict well in somewhat unexpected courses; it provides fairly good forecasting of grades in English, social studies, mechanical drawing, languages and even typing. Since the content of the test seems unrelated to the nature of these courses, one can only surmise that the reasoning process it draws upon is an aspect of scholastic ability which is useful in many academic learnings.

From *Personnel and Guidance Journal*, 1952, *31*, 167-170. Copyright 1952 American Personnel and Guidance Association. Reprinted with permission.

Another generalization is that the course grades of girls are more predictable than those of boys. Though it may not be true of individual classes, the greater predictability of girls' grades is remarkably consistent when we inspect summaries of validity studies of the Differential Aptitude Tests. It holds for courses such as mathematics and science, which are usually associated with boys, as well as for English and social studies. Why this should be so may provoke interesting conjecture, but the research done thus far has not provided any clues; we know only that it is so.

Perhaps one of the most important demonstrations provided by the thousands of validity coefficients is that of the specificity of validity. Though lip service is often paid to this principle in textbooks, all too many test manuals still report single validity coefficients for a course or occupation as though that one coefficient really represented the validity which other users of the test might expect. How far wrong such an implication is likely to be may be illustrated from any of the summary tables in the DAT manual. For example, the manual reports 29 coefficients between English grades and DAT Verbal Reasoning for boys. The highest of these validity coefficients is 0.78; the lowest is 0.19. If either of these values were the only information provided, it would be quite misleading to other users of the test. The median coefficients of 0.48 based on 29 separate studies of boys and of 0.54 based on 24 separate studies of girls, are much more dependable estimates of the probable validity of the test in new situations.

Why This Wide Range?

What brings about this wide range of validity coefficients — why is validity so specific? Several causes quickly appear as we consider the problem. The most important of these is obviously the different nature of the courses taught under the same name. We speak of twenty-nine English courses — but some of these may be concerned primarily with grammar and the mechanics of the language, while others are courses in literary appreciation or creative composition. We speak of predicting mathematics grades, but the actual courses vary from general mathematics, with stress on arithmetic computation skill and problems of interest and profit calculation to advanced algebra, solid geometry and trigonometry calling for high level appreciation of abstract mathematical symbolism. Science courses may mean descriptive facts in biology, the balancing of equations in chemistry or the complex interrelations of forces in physics. To expect any test to predict in the same way the performance of students in courses which make such different demands on the abilities of students is unreasonable.

Another reason for variability of the validity coefficients is the variability of the students being studied. In some schools, all students in a given grade are exposed to the same course. In other schools, students are sectioned according to previous performance in earlier courses, performance on aptitude or similar tests, or curricular goals such as academic, commercial or industrial arts.

The very fact of sectioning serves to narrow the range of talent in a course and depress the size of the validity coefficient. Sectioning also serves to induce different course content for the different students with the effects noted above. A third effect of sectioning is to make grades less meaningful from section to section, further confounding attempts at prediction for the group as a whole. A student who is in the best section may be graded "B" for greater knowledge and ability than is possessed by an "A" student in the poorest section. The aptitude test score achieved by the former student is likely to be higher than that of the student in the poor section. When the aptitude scores, based on absolute test performance, are correlated with course grades based on achievement relative to a good group for some students and relative to a poor group for other students, validity coefficients are inevitably depressed. So it is that while sectioning may be a desirable plan of academic organization, it raises havoc with validity studies.

Sectioning is not the only cause for ambiguity in grades. The age-old tendency of teachers to reward students for promptness, neatness, cooperation and similar virtues which are only partially related to real achievement of academic knowledge and skills is well known. Equally recognized over the years has been the often inadequate reliability of school grades.

A section of the DAT manual devoted to studies of the prediction of achievement as measured by tests rather than grades provides evidence of the higher validity coefficients to be anticipated when achievement tests are the criteria. For example, in one such study where the Iowa Tests of Educational Development were administered to tenth, eleventh, and twelfth grade boys and girls who had taken the DAT a year earlier, the Verbal Reasoning test predicted social studies scores to the extent of 0.70, 0.75, 0.57, 0.78, 0.79, and 0.85. Five of the six validity coefficients for Numerical Ability against Quantitative Thinking were 0.80 or higher. One seldom finds validity coefficients of this magnitude for any tests when course grades are the criteria.

DAT Follow-Up

One of the most ambitious tasks undertaken with the DAT was the follow-up into later careers of some 1,800 students who had been tested as eleventh or twelfth graders.[1] Profiles were developed for those who had successfully progressed in a number of educational curricula (engineering, liberal arts, business administration, etc.) or had been employed as salesmen, electricians, clerks, stenographers, telephone operators, or at

---

[1]G.K. Bennett, H.G. Seashore, and A.G. Wesman, "Aptitude Testing: Does It 'Prove Out' in Counseling Practice?" *Occupations* XXX (May, 1952), 584-593.

several other occupations. Success was defined minimally for this study as being represented by the student's having spent two or more years at the course or job and having expressed the intention of continuing in the same direction. The profiles typical of students entering each of these careers provide, the author feels, highly significant information to the high school counselor. For the most part, the average profiles support the present practices of counselors. Engineering students were strong in Numerical Ability and outstanding in Mechanical Reasoning and Space Relations; of all employed female groups, stenographers were clearly best in Spelling. An equally important conclusion is that within any one career group there may be found a wide range of talent. The counselor advising the individual student obviously needs all the relevant data he can obtain; he dare not be swayed only by average profiles, nor judge by test results alone. As a description of the competition the student will face, however, these average profiles can contribute much to ultimate decisions.

Using Early Test Results

Can career counseling make use of early aptitude test results, or is it necessary to wait until the student is almost ready to leave the high school? This question involves not only the reliability of tests but also the constancy of the aptitudes being measured. If the student's relative standing on the tests changes appreciably between his ninth and twelfth grades, short-term high school counseling is possible, but long-range career counseling based on the tests is not feasible. If, on the other hand, the student's performance is relatively stable, long-term planning may be undertaken with greater confidence. Considerable constancy of performance was found in a study[2] in which students who had taken the DAT in the ninth grade were retested in the twelfth grade. Despite different kinds and amounts of practice — in and outside of schools — in the abilities measured by the tests, the students maintained their relative ranks quite well (range of uncorrected $r=0.58$ to 0.87; median $r=0.72$). This fact speaks well for the stability with which the tests are measuring, and permits the counselor to think in long-range terms as well as to consider immediate goals.

One way of learning to understand the nature of a test is to correlate performance on it and other tests. DAT scores have been correlated with scores on several intelligence, aptitude and achievement tests to provide this kind of information. Perhaps the most provocative of such studies, however, was one concerned with the correlation of the DAT and the Kuder Preference Record in the tenth, eleventh, and twelfth grades.[3]

---

[2]J.E. Doppelt and G.K. Bennett, "A Longitudinal Study of the Differential Aptitude Tests," *Educational and Psychological Measurement*, XI (1951), 228-237.

[3]G.K. Bennett, H.G. Seashore, and A.G. Wesman, *Differential Aptitude Tests Manual*. New York: The Psychological Corporation, 1947, pp. E-85, E-92-3.

Since the results were analyzed separately for boys and girls in each of the three grades, six tables of intercorrelations were prepared. An inspection of these tables reveals only two appropriate pairings — DAT Mechanical Reasoning and Kuder Mechanical and Science Interest — which show a consistent and significant relationship, and these hold only for boys. For no other pairings — relevant as well as irrelevant — are the coefficients consistently significant. Experienced counselors may not need the reminder these data contain; to less experienced counselors, the results may well serve as a warning not to base counseling on interest scores without positive information with respect to the appropriate aptitudes and abilities of the student.

How are the Differential Aptitude Tests used? Anyone can learn from the practices of his colleagues, and experience with DAT has been no exception to this truism. The more obvious ways have already been implied in the foregoing discussion: the tests are used by counselors for the prediction of academic success and the guidance of students into appropriate courses and careers; they provide the student with a clearer idea of his abilities and those of the competition he is likely to meet in high school, and some post-high school, careers. Several other uses are perhaps of equal interest, though less often made.

Placement officers have improved their relations with industrial personnel men by recommending students with greater likelihood of success. Combining the knowledge concerning the students' DAT performances with the other available information about the students permits the counselor to recommend better qualified students to industry, and to suggest more appropriate jobs to students about to seek employment. When the personnel man has himself become familiar with the DAT, he can specify the kind of student he is seeking with more precise descriptions.

A significant contribution to educational practice has been the utilization of the DAT in curriculum research. The traditional approach to framing a curriculum has been based on a frequently unformulated philosophy of education contemplating the needs of the abstract future citizen. Those systems which offer nothing but classical education to students whose goals do not, and often cannot, envision a college education, are adhering to this practice. A far more fruitful approach is to take into account the needs of students in the community, and to base the curriculum on those needs, and on the abilities which are the students' potential assets. To require a future garage mechanic or carpenter to take several years of Latin and French seems futile; to deprive him of the opportunity to take automotive or woodworking courses is worse than futile — it is unfair to the student and the community. Several school systems have recently come to this point of view. They have surveyed the aptitudes of their students through grade-wide administration of the DAT and are proceeding to use the results, together with information as to students' goals and job opportunities in their communities, to revise their curricula accordingly. Other school systems may well follow their enlightened example.

Another kind of student rescued in part because of DAT profiles has been one who needs bolstering in his self-regard. Students with unfortunate early educational experiences often accept the role of being retarded, and give up serious efforts to learn new materials. Typically they set goals for themselves which are beneath their potential — which represents wasted talent for student and community alike. Many such students, when shown by a sympathetic counselor a profile indicating some demonstrated strengths, are readier to re-evaluate their goals and approach education with greater confidence. A number of counselors have reported such experiences with well-justified feelings of gratification.

It will be obvious that not all of the uses which have been made of the DAT have been recited here. The tests are tools which provide counselors and students with certain kinds of information. How that information will be utilized depends on the problems of the individual students and the wisdom of the individual counselor, school administrator or psychologist. The five years of experience have demonstrated that the tests can be useful in predicting the student's progress, and can provide significant details for an inventory of the student's strengths and weaknesses in some important traits. When these facts are combined with a record of the student's previous achievement, his hopes for the future, and the other important information which the student, his family and the school can provide, ability to help the student progress toward reasonable, satisfying goals has been appreciably enhanced.

Faking Personality Test Scores in a Simulated Employment Situation

It has been the experience of most industrial psychologists that personality and interest inventories are ineffective when used for selection purposes (1,2,3,4,6,7,8). Ordinarily, many of the items can be seen through by most applicants, and the appropriate response given. The stereotypes which many employment officers seek (e.g., aggressive, self-confident salesmen) are also the stereotypes which the applicant expects the employer to be seeking. He is therefore all too likely to respond accordingly.

The data reported herein were collected in the course of a teaching demonstration. The author wished to impress a group of extension students at a large university with the untrustworthiness of personality inventories in employee selection. He gave the Bernreuter Personality Inventory to a group of 85 students with about the following instructions:

> "I want you to pretend that you are applying for the position of salesman in a large industrial organization. You have been unemployed for some time, have a family to support, and want very much to land this position. You are being given this test by the employment manager. Please mark the answers you would give."

The following week, at the start of class, the same inventory was again distributed to the class, with the following instructions:

> "You are now applying for the position of librarian in a small town. You need the employment to support your family and meet financial obligations. Please mark the answers you would give."

Both administrations of the inventory occurred before there was any discussion of the field of personality measurement. The 73 students who took the test twice were a very heterogeneous group in age, academic background, industrial experience, and test sophistication. On the latter variable, they ranged from a young lady taking her first course since high school, with almost complete innocence of the test field, to a young man about to receive a Ph. D. in measurement, with several years of professional experience behind him.

Table I presents the score distributions obtained from these two

TABLE I. Students' Scores on a Self-Confidence Scale in Two Simulated Employment Situations

Self-Confidence Scale	Employment Situation	
	Salesman	Librarian
Raw Score*		
260-241	1	
240-221	2	
220-201	18	
200-181	27	7
180-161	11	3
160-141	2	6
140-121	4	3
120-101	2	6
100- 81	1	8
80- 61	2	3
60- 41		3
40- 21		
20- 1		
0- 19	2	3
20- 39		3
40- 59		1
60- 79		2
80- 99		3
100-119		4
120-139		4
140-159		1
160-179		4
180-199		2
200-219		1
220-239		2
240-259		3
260-279		1
280-299	1	
Total	73	73

The left margin labels read: "Minus Values" for the upper block (Raw Score 260-241 through 20- 1) and "Plus Values" for the lower block (0- 19 through 280-299).

*Minus scores represent greater self-confidence.

administrations of the inventory for one of the measured traits, Self-Confidence (Scale F-1) (5). The table speaks eloquently for itself. If one saw these distributions without foreknowledge of how they were obtained, he could only conclude that they represented two quite different groups of people. The first column, "Salesman," is apparently composed of people who are, with three exceptions, above average in self-confidence. The second group, "Librarian," seems to contain almost as many below-average people on this trait as above-average (34 and 39, respectively). Those at the *fifth* percentile of the first group are more self-confident than the "applicants" at the *fiftieth* percentile of the second group. It is hard to realize that these "two" groups are really one and the same, except that the positions for which they are pretending to apply are different.

The demonstration is, of course, artificial. These are not true applicants. They are students pretending that they are applicants. Unquestionably, some of them are more test-wise (and stereotype-wise) than the average real applicant. Nonetheless, the demonstration seems to the author sufficiently dramatic to point up the susceptibility to faking of personality inventories in the industrial situations. Teachers who have not already used similar demonstrations with their students will find this approach rewarding.

References

1. Benton, A.L., and Kornhauser, G.I. A study of "score faking" on a medical interest test. *J. Ass. Amer. Med. Coll.*, 1948, **23**, 57-60.

2. Bordin, E.S. A theory of vocational interests as dynamic phenomena. *Educ. psychol. Measmt.*, 1943, 3, 49-65.

3. Cofer, C.N., Chance, June, and Judson, A.J. A study of malingering on the MMPI. *J. Psychol.*, 1949, **27**, 491-499.

4. Ellis, A. The validity of personality questionnaires. *Psychol. Bull.*, 1946, **43**, 385-440.

5. Flanagan, J.C. *Factor analysis in the study of personality.* Stanford: Stanford University Press, 1935, Pp. 103.

6. Hunt, H.F. The effect of deliberate deception on Minnesota Multiphasic Personality Inventory performance. *J. consult. Psychol.*, 1948, **12**, 396-402.

7. Longstaff, H.P. Fakability of the Strong Interest Blank and the Kuder Preference Record. *J. appl. Psychol.*, 1948, **32**, 360-369.

8. Paterson, D.G. Vocational interest inventories in selection. *Occupations*, 1946, **25**, 152-153.

Reliability and Confidence

The chief purpose of testing is to permit us to arrive at judgments concerning the people being tested. If those judgments are to have any real merit, they must be based on dependable scores — which, in turn, must be earned on dependable tests. If our measuring instrument is unreliable, any judgments based on it are necessarily of doubtful worth. No one would consider relying on a thermometer which gave readings varying from 96° to 104° for persons known to have normal temperatures. Nor would any of us place confidence in measurements of length based on an elastic ruler. While few tests are capable of yielding scores which are as dependable as careful measurements of length obtained by use of a well-marked (and rigid!) ruler, we seek in tests some satisfactory amount of dependability — of "rely-ability."

It is a statistical and logical fact that no test can be valid unless it is reliable; knowing the reliability of a test in a particular situation, we know the limits beyond which validity in that situation cannot rise. Knowing reliability, we know also how large a band of error surrounds a test score — how precisely or loosely that score can be interpreted. In view of the importance of the concept of reliability, it is unfortunate that so many inadequacies in the reporting and use of reliability coefficients are to be found in the literature. This article is intended to clarify some aspects of this very fundamental characteristic of tests.

Reliability coefficients are designed to provide estimates of the consistency or precision of measurements. When used with psychological tests, the coefficients may serve one or both of two purposes: (1) to estimate the precision of the test itself as a measuring instrument, or (2) to estimate the consistency of the examinees' performances on the test. The second kind of reliability obviously embraces the first. We can have

From *Test Service Bulletin* No. 44, The Psychological Corporation, 1952.

unreliable behavior by the examinee on a relatively reliable test, but we cannot have reliable performance on an unreliable instrument. A student or applicant suffering a severe headache may give an uncharacteristic performance on a well-built test; the test may be reliable, but the subject's performance is not typical of him. If, however, the test items are ambiguous, the directions are unclear, or the pictures are so poorly reproduced as to be unintelligible — if, in short, the test materials are themselves inadequate — the subject is prevented from performing reliably, however propitious his mental and physical condition.

This two-fold purpose of reliability coefficients is reflected in the several methods which have been developed for estimating reliability. Methods which provide estimates based on a single sitting offer evidence as to the precision of the test itself; these include internal consistency estimates, such as those obtained by use of the split-half and Kuder-Richardson techniques when the test is given only once, as well as estimates based on immediate retesting, whether with the same form or an equivalent one. When a time interval of one or more days is introduced, so that day-to-day variability in the person taking the test is allowed to have an effect, we have evidence concerning the stability of the trait and of the examinee as well as of the test. It is important to recognize whether a reliability coefficient describes only the test, or whether it describes the stability of the examinees' performances as well.

How High Should a Reliability Coefficient Be?

We should naturally like to have as much consistency in our measuring instruments as the physicist and the chemist achieve. However, the complexities of human personality and other practical considerations often place limits on the accuracy with which we measure and we accept reliability coefficients of different sizes depending on various purposes and situations. Perhaps the most important of these considerations is the gravity of the decision to be made on the basis of the test score. The psychologist who has to recommend whether or not a person is to be committed to an institution is obligated to seek the most reliable instruments he can obtain. The counselor inquiring as to whether a student is likely to do better in one curriculum or another may settle for a slightly less reliable instrument, but his demands should still be high. A survey of parents' attitudes towards school practices needs only moderate reliability, since only the *average* or group figures need to be highly dependable and not the specific responses of individual parents. Test constructors experimenting with ideas for tests may accept rather low reliability in the early stages of experimentation — those tests which show promise can then be built up into more reliable instruments before publication.

It is much like the question of how confident we wish to be about decisions in other areas of living. The industrial organization about to hire a top executive (whose decisions may seriously affect the entire business) will usually spend large sums of time and money to obtain reliable evidence concerning a candidate's qualifications for the job. The same firm will devote far less time or money to the hiring of a clerk or office boy, whose errors are of lesser consequence. In buying a house, we want to have as much confidence in our decision as we can reasonably get. In buying a package of razor blades, slim evidence is sufficient since we lose little if we have to throw away the entire package or replace it sooner than expected. The principle is simply stated: the more important the decision to be reached, the greater is our need for confidence in the precision of the test and the higher is the required reliability coefficient.

Two Factors Affecting the Interpretation of Reliability Coefficients

Actually, there is no such thing as *the* reliability coefficient for a test. Like validity, reliability is specific to the group on which it is estimated. The reliability coefficient will be higher in one situation than in another according to circumstances which may or may not reflect real differences in the precision of measurement. Among these factors are the range of ability in the group and the interval of time between testings.

Range of talent

If a reliability estimate is based on a group which has a small spread in the ability measured by the test, the coefficient will be relatively low. If the group is one which has a wide range in that particular talent, the coefficient will be higher. That is, the reliability coefficient will vary with the range of talent in the group, even though the accuracy of measurement is unchanged. The following example may illustrate how this comes about. For simplicity, we have used small numbers of cases; ordinarily, far larger groups would be required to ensure a coefficient in which we could have confidence.

In Table I are shown the raw scores and rankings of twenty students on two forms of an arithmetic test. Looking at the two sets of rankings, we see that changes in rank from one form to the other are minor; the ranks shift a little, but not importantly. A coefficient computed from these data would be fairly high.

Now, however, let us examine only the rankings of the five top students. Though for these five students the shifts in rank are the same as before, the importance of the shifts is greatly emphasized. Whereas in the larger group student C's change in rank from third to fifth represented only a ten per cent shift (two places out of twenty), his shift of two places in rank in the

TABLE I. Raw Scores and Ranks of Students on Two Forms of an Arithmetic Test

Student	Form X		Form Y	
	Score	Rank	Score	Rank
A	90	1	88	2
B	87	2	89	1
C	83	3	76	5
D	78	4	77	4
E	72	5	80	3
F	70	6	65	7
G	68	7	64	8
H	65	8	67	6
I	60	9	53	10
J	54	10	57	9
K	51	11	49	11
L	47	12	45	14
M	46	13	48	12
N	43	14	47	13
O	39	15	44	15
P	38	16	42	16
Q	32	17	39	17
R	30	18	34	20
S	29	19	37	18
T	25	20	36	19

smaller top group is a forty per cent change (two places out of five). When the entire twenty represent the group on which we estimate the reliability of the arithmetic test, going from third on form X to fifth on form Y still leaves the student as one of the best in this population. If, on the other hand, reliability is being estimated only on the group consisting of the top five students, going from third to fifth means dropping from the middle to the bottom of this population — a radical change. A coefficient, if computed for just these five cases, would be quite low.

Note that it is not the smaller number of cases which brings about the lower coefficient. It is the narrower range of talent which is responsible. A coefficient based on five cases as widespread as the twenty (e.g., pupils A,E,J,O, and T, who rank first, fifth, tenth, fifteenth, and twentieth respectively on form X), would be at least as large as the coefficient based on all twenty students.

This example shows why the reliability coefficient may vary even though the test questions and the stability of the students' performances are unchanged. A test may discriminate with satisfactory precision among students with wide ranges of talent but not discriminate equally well in a narrow range of talent. A yardstick is unsatisfactory if we must differentiate objects varying in length from 35.994 to 36.008 inches. Reliability coefficients reflect this fact, which holds regardless of the kind of reliability coefficient computed. It should be obvious, then, that *no reliability coefficient can be properly interpreted without information as to the spread of ability in the group on which it is based.* A reliability coefficient of .65 based on a narrow range of talent is fully as good as a coefficient of .90 based on a group with twice that spread of scores. Reliability coefficients are very much a function of the range of talent in the group.

Interval between testings

When two forms of a test are taken at a single sitting, the reliability coefficient computed by correlating the two forms is likely to overestimate somewhat the real accuracy of the test. This is so because factors such as mental set, physical condition of examinees, conditions of test administration, etc.— factors which are irrelevant to the test itself — are likely to operate equally on both forms, thus making each person's pair of scores more similar than they otherwise would be. The same type of overestimate may be expected when reliability is computed by split-half or other internal consistency techniques, which are based on a single test administration. Coefficients such as these describe the accuracy of the test, but exaggerate the practical accuracy of the results by the extent to which the examinees and the testing situation may normally be expected to fluctuate. As indicated above, coefficients based on a single sitting do not describe the stability of the subjects' performances.

When we set out to investigate how stable the test results are likely to be from day to day or week to week, we are likely to underestimate the test's accuracy, though we may succeed in obtaining a realistic estimate of stability of the examinees' performances on the test. The underestimation of the test's accuracy depends on the extent to which changes in the examinees have taken place between testings. The same influences mentioned above — mental set, physical condition of examinees, and the like — which *increase* coefficients based on a single sitting are likely to *decrease* coefficients when testing is done on different days. It is unlikely for example, that the same persons who had headaches the first day will also have headaches on the day of the second testing.

Changes in the persons tested may also be of a kind directly related to the content of the particular test. If a month has elapsed between two administrations of an arithmetic test, different pupils may have learned different amounts of arithmetic during the interval. The second testing should then show greater score increases for those who learned more than for those who learned less. The correlation coefficient under these conditions will reflect the test's accuracy *minus* the effect of differential learning; it will not really be a reliability coefficient.

For most educational and industrial purposes, the reliability coefficient which reflects *stability of performance* over a relatively short time is the more important. Usually, we wish to know whether the student or job applicant would have achieved a similar score if he had been tested on some other day, or whether he might have shown up quite differently. It would be unfortunate and unfair to make important decisions on the basis of test results which might have been quite different had the person been tested the day before or a day later. We want an estimate of reliability which takes into account accidental changes in day-to-day ability of the individual, but which has not been affected by real learning between testings. Such a reliability coefficient would be based on two sittings, separated by one or more days so that day-to-day changes are reflected in the scores, but not separated by so much time that permanent changes, or learning, have occurred.[1] Two forms of a test, administered a day to a week apart, would usually satisfy these conditions. If the same form of a test is used in both sittings, the intervening time should be long enough to minimize the role of memory from the first to the second administrations.

Ideally, then, our reliability coefficient would ordinarily be based on two different but equivalent forms of the test, administered to a group on two separate occasions. However, it is often not feasible to meet these conditions: there may be only one form of the test available, or the group may be available for only one day, or the test may be one which is itself a learning experience. We are then forced to rely on coefficients based on a single administration. Fortunately, when such coefficients are properly used they usually provide close approximations to the estimates which would have been obtained with alternate forms administered at different times.

Some Common Misconceptions

Reliability of speed tests

Although estimates of reliability based on one administration of the test are often satisfactory, there are some circumstances in which *only* retest methods are proper. Most notable is the case in which we are dealing with an easy test given under speed conditions. If the test is composed of items which almost anyone can answer correctly given enough time but which most people tested cannot finish in the time allowed, the test is largely a

---

[1] A coefficient which is based on two testings between which opportunity for learning has occurred is a useful statistic. It may provide evidence of how much individual variation in learning has taken place, or of the stability of the knowledge, skills or aptitudes being measured. It is similar to a reliability coefficient, and is in part a function of the reliability of the two measurements; but such a coefficient should not be interpreted as simply estimating reliability – it requires a more complex interpretation.

measure of speed. Many clerical and simple arithmetic tests used with adults are examples of speed tests. Internal consistency methods, whether they are of the Kuder-Richardson or of the split-half type, provide false and often grossly exaggerated estimates of the reliability of such tests. To demonstrate this problem, two forms of a simple but speed-laden clerical test were given to a group. For *each* form the odd-even (split-half) reliability coefficient was found to be over .99. However, when scores on Form A were correlated with scores on Form B, the coefficient was .88. This latter value is a more accurate estimate of the reliability of the test.[2] Many equally dramatic illustrations of how spurious an inappropriate coefficient can be may be found readily, even in manuals for professionally made tests.

If a test is somewhat dependent on speed, but the items range in difficulty from easy to hard, internal consistency estimates will not be as seriously misleading as when the test items are simple and the test is highly speeded. As the importance of speed diminishes, these estimates will be less different from the coefficients which would be obtained by retest methods. It is difficult to guess how far wrong an inappropriate coefficient for a speeded test is. *Whenever there is evidence that speed is important in test performance, the safest course is to insist on an estimate of reliability based on test-and-retest,* if necessary with the same but preferably with an alternate form of the test.

Part vs. total reliability

Some of the tests we use are composed of several parts which are individually scored and the part scores are then added to yield a total score. Often, reliability is reported only for the total score, with no information given as to the reliability of the scores on the individual parts. This may lead to seriously mistaken assumptions regarding the reliability of the part scores — and, thus, of the confidence we may place in judgments based on the part scores. The longer a test is, other things being equal, the more reliable it is; the shorter the test, the lower is its reliability likely to be. A part score based on only a portion of the items in a test can hardly be expected to be as reliable as the total score; if we treat the part score as though it has the reliability of the total score, we misplace our confidence — sometimes quite seriously.

As an example, we may look at the Wechsler Intelligence Scale for Children, one of the most important instruments of its kind. Five subtests are combined to yield a total Verbal Score for this test. The reliability coefficient for the Verbal Score, based on 200 representative ten-year-olds, is .96 — high enough to warrant considerable confidence in the accuracy of

---

[2]Manual for the *Differential Aptitude Tests*, Revised Edition, page 65. The Psychological Corporation, 1952.

measurement for these youngsters. For the same population, however, a single subtest (General Comprehension) yields a reliability coefficient of only .73 — a far less impressive figure. If we allow ourselves to act as though the total test reliability coefficient of .96 represents the consistency of measurement we can expect from the Comprehension subtest, we are likely to encounter unpleasant surprises on future retests. More importantly, any clinical judgments which ignore the relatively poor reliability of the part score are dangerous. Test users should consider it a basic rule that *if evidence of adequate reliability for part scores is missing, the part scores should not be used.*

Reliability for what group?

This question may be considered as a special case under the principles discussed above with respect to range of talent. It is worth special consideration because it is so often ignored. Even the best documented of test manuals present only limited numbers of reliability coefficients; in too many manuals a single coefficient is all that is made available. On what group should a reliability coefficient be based?

When we interpret an individual's test score, the most meaningful reliability coefficient is one based on the group with which the individual is competing. Stated otherwise, the most appropriate group is that in which the counselor, clinician or employment manager is trying to make decisions

Each of us is a member of many groups

as to the relative ability of the individuals on the trait being measured. Any one person is, of course, a member of many groups. An applicant for a job may also be classified as a high school or college graduate, an experienced or inexperienced salesman or bookkeeper, a local or out-of-state person, a member of one political party or another, below or above age thirty, etc. A high school student is a boy or girl; a member of an academic, trade or commercial school group; a member of an English class, a geometry class, or a woodworking or cooking class; a freshman or a junior; a future engineer or nurse or garage mechanic. Obviously, it would be impossible for a test manual to offer reliability for *all* the groups of which any one individual is a member.

The appropriate group is represented by the individual's present competition. If we are testing applicants for clerical work, the most meaningful reliability coefficient is one based on applicants for clerical work. Coefficients based on employed clerical workers are somewhat less useful, those based on high school graduates are still less useful; as we go on to *more general* groups — e.g., all high school students or all adults — the coefficients become less and less meaningful. Similarly, as we go to *less relevant* groups (even though they may be quite specific) the reliability coefficients are also less relevant and less meaningful. The reliability of a test calculated on the basis of mechanical apprentices, college sophomores, or junior executives reveals little of importance when we are concerned with clerical applicants. What we need to know is how well the test discriminates among applicants for clerical work. If we can define the population with even greater specificity and relevance — e.g., female applicants for filing jobs — so much the better. *The closer the resemblance between the group on which the reliability coefficient is based and the group of individuals about whose relative ability we need to decide, the more meaningful is that coefficient of reliability.*

Test reliability vs. scorer reliability

Some tests are not entirely objective as to scoring method; the scorer is required to make a judgment as to the correctness or quality of the response. This is frequently true in individually-administered tests (Wechsler or Binet for example), projective techniques in personality measurement (Rorschach, Sentence Completion, etc.) and many other tests in which the subject is asked to supply the answer, rather than to select one of several stated choices. For tests such as these, it is important to know the extent of agreement between the persons who score them. Test manuals usually report the amount of agreement by means of a coefficient of correlation between scores assigned to a set of test papers by two or more independent scorers.

Such a correlation coefficient yields important information — it tells us how objectively the test can be scored. It even contributes some evidence of reliability, since objectivity of scoring is a factor which makes for test reliability. Such a coefficient should not, however, be considered a reliability coefficient for the test; it is only an estimate of *scoring* reliability — a statement of how much confidence we may have that two scorers will arrive at similar scores for a given test paper. Moreover, it is possible for a test to be quite unreliable as a measuring instrument, yet have high scoring objectivity. We should remember that many objective tests — those in which the person selects one of several stated options — are not very reliable, yet the scoring is by definition objective. A short personality inventory may have a retest reliability coefficient of .20; but if it is the usual paper-and-pencil set of questions with a clear scoring key, two scorers should agree perfectly, except for clerical errors, in assigning scores to the test. The coefficient of correlation between their sets of scores might well be 1.00.

In short, information as to scorer agreement is important but not sufficient. The crucial question — How precisely is the test measuring the individual? — is not answered by scorer agreement; a real reliability coefficient is required.

A Practical Check-List

When reading a test manual, the test user would do well to apply a mental check-list to the reliability section, raising at least the following questions for each reliability coefficient:

1. What does the coefficient measure?
   a. Precision of the test — coefficient based on single sitting?
   b. Stability of examinees' test performances — coefficient based on test-and-retest with a few days intervening?
2. Is it more than a reliability coefficient? .... does it also measure constancy of the trait? .... is the coefficient based on test-and-retest with enough intervening time for learning or similar changes to have occurred?
3. Do scores on the test depend largely on how rapidly the examinees can answer the questions? If so, is the reliability coefficient based on a test-and-retest study?
4. Are there part scores intended for consideration separately? If so, is each part score reliable enough to warrant my confidence?
5. Is the group on which this coefficient is based appropriate to my purpose? Does it consist of people similar to those with whom I shall be using the test?
6. Since a reliability coefficient, like any other statistic, requires a reasonable number of cases to be itself dependable, how large is the group on which the coefficient is based?

If, and *only* if, the coefficients can be accepted as meeting the above standards, one may ask:

7. In view of the importance of the judgments I shall make, is the correlation coefficient large enough to warrant my use of the test?

A reliability coefficient is a statistic — simply a number which summarizes a relationship. Before it takes on meaning, its reader must understand the logic of the study from which the coefficient was derived, the nature of the coefficient and the forces which affect it. Statistics may reveal or conceal — what they do depends to a very large extent on the logical ability and awareness the reader brings to them. Figures do lie, to those who don't or won't understand them.

Better than Chance

"Tests with a coefficient of validity less than .50 are practically useless, except in distinguishing between extreme cases, since at that value of r the forecasting efficiency is only 13.4 per cent."[1] This statement is quoted from one of the leading statistical texts; its paraphrase may be found in many other texts, in doctoral dissertations and other treatises of greater or lesser authority. But relatively few validity coefficients, especially in industry, exceed .50.

Why are tests being used even though they generally fall into this "practically useless" class? Is it because of ignorance on the part of test users? Not at all. Witness the statement by the author of the above quotation in reviewing a test with validity coefficients averaging .35 to .55 in various institutions: "[the test] has shown substantial value in predicting scholarship at the graduate level."[2] Now the forecasting efficiency (using the same formula as was used above) even when $r = .55$ is about 16 per cent — hardly enough to warrant the author's shift from condemnation to commendation. The reader might justifiably be confused — if the expert can't agree with himself, what is the counselor or personnel man to think?

Reassurance is in order. The test user may follow the practice of the expert, without violating the principle enunciated in the texts. The "index of forecasting efficiency" as formulated in the texts is concerned with a precision of prediction much finer than that required in most practical situations. As a measure of the real utility of a test, the index may be grossly misleading. A more crucial consideration is the extent to which broader judgments are improved.

The difference between the two concepts can be seen clearly if we consider the prediction, in two different situations, of how far several men

From *Test Service Bulletin* No. 45, The Psychological Corporation, 1953.

[1]References denoted by superscript numbers will be found at the end of this article.

can broadjump. If the occasion is an athletic contest, we might want to predict just how many feet and inches each man will cover. The average difference between our estimated distances and the actual jumps will serve as a crude indicator of our predictive efficiency – the better (i.e., the more valid) the basis on which we make our predictions, the smaller this average difference will become, and the percentage by which it decreases is analogous to the per cent of improvement over chance. But suppose we move from the athletic contest or theoretical laboratory situation to one in which the practical values are extreme: say, one in which it's necessary to leap across a brook. Those who fail by inches to make it will get their feet wet as will those who miss by six feet. And those who just clear it will be as useful on the other side as those who sail over with five feet to spare. *Now* the test of the efficiency of our predictive test lies in the confidence with which it permits us to say, "of men who score like this, nine out of ten will make it, but of those whose scores are the lowest only three out of ten will get across." Of course, the absolute dichotomy is as extreme in its way as the pinpoint precision estimate is at the other extreme. But when we are trying to guess in which general category, high, middle or low – the champions, the experts, the good, the just average, or the duffers – our candidates will fall, we're closer to the second situation than the first. Most counselors, personnel men, and clinicians have to work with these cruder approximations.

Per cent of improvement over chance, as used with the index of forecasting efficiency, refers to the narrowing of a zone of error around a predicted score. When the validity coefficient is zero, knowledge of a test score does not permit us to predict an individual's score on the criterion with any accuracy at all; the best guess we can make with respect to any individual, regardless of how he scored on such a test, is that he will be average on the criterion. The band of error (the standard error of estimate) is as large as the spread (the standard deviation) of the ratings on the criterion for the entire group. As the correlation between the test scores and the criterion ratings increases, our precision in predicting ratings of individuals on the criterion also increases and we may predict with some degree of confidence, for example, that a person who scores in the top quarter on the test will be rated in the top quarter on the criterion as well. Of course, some of our predictions will be in error: i.e., some of those whose scores are in the top quarter on the test will be rated in the second quarter on performance, a smaller number in the third quarter, and a few may even be rated in the lowest quarter. The larger the validity coefficient, the fewer misplaced persons there will be; furthermore, the smaller will be the amount of displacement. In other words, if the validity coefficient is really high, we may expect most of those who score in the top quarter on the test to be rated in the top quarter on performance as well, a very few to be rated in the second quarter, and fewer still (or perhaps even none at all) to be rated in the third or fourth quarters.

The number of persons for whom statistically calculated predictions are wrong, and the amount by which our estimates are in error are reflected in the *standard error of estimate*. When validity is perfect, the standard error of estimate is zero; when validity is zero, the standard error of estimate is at its maximum. As the validity increases, the standard error of estimate decreases. The degree to which the standard error of estimate is reduced is what is meant by the textbook statements concerning improvement over chance. In this sense, large validity coefficients are necessary; it takes an $r = .866$ to cut the standard error of estimate even to half the size of the standard deviation of the criterion ratings – a "fifty per cent improvement over chance."

What permits us to use tests effectively even though their validity coefficients are considerably lower than .866? First, there is the matter of precision. The standard error of estimate refers to the band of error around predictions of precise, specific rankings of each individual on the criterion. In most practical work, such precision is unnecessary. We do not ordinarily need to predict that John Jones will be exactly at the 85th percentile in a college class, or that Bill Smith will be 19th in a group of 25 engineering apprentices. We are far more likely to be concerned with whether Jones will survive the first year in college, or whether Smith will be one of the satisfactory apprentices. For these purposes, whether Jones is at the 75th percentile or 90th percentile is of lesser moment; we can make a quite confident prediction that he will succeed, even though there may be a fair-sized standard error of estimate applicable to the specific percentile our formula predicts.

A second factor working in our favor in the practical use of tests is that, as the opening quotation notes, predictions are most accurately made at the extremes – and it is the extremes that are of greatest interest to us. Few colleges grant large scholarships to more than 10 or 20 per cent of their students. Few colleges fail as many as half their students and few industrial firms fire as many as half of those they hire. More often, the failures are 10 per cent or 20 per cent or possibly 30 per cent – the extremes. Thus a test which does not predict with accuracy whether students will be at the 40th percentile or the 60th percentile can still do a valuable service in predicting that very few of the high scorers will be in the 20 per cent who fail during the freshman year, or that hardly any scholarship winners will be academic failures. In industrial selection, a test of moderate validity can be efficient in quickly screening out the "clearly ineligible" from the "clearly eligible." There will remain an indifferent zone of test scores for persons in the "eligible" range; for them, other considerations than test scores may determine whether they should be hired.

Let us look at some data. One hundred ninety-one eighth-grade boys took the *Verbal Reasoning Test* of the *Differential Aptitude Tests (DAT)* battery at the start of a term. At the end of the term, the grades they earned in a Social Studies course were obtained. Seventy-six were found to have earned grades of D or lower; they represented 40 per cent of the total class. On the basis of chance (i.e., using a test with *zero* validity), we should expect to find that 40 per cent of those at each test score level – low, medium or high – obtained grades of D or lower. The coefficient of correlation between the test scores and these grades was .61, for which the index of forecasting efficiency comes out to just 20 per cent better than chance – hardly enough to notice. Table I reveals a very different story – it shows the test to be a highly efficient predictor for the school's purposes!

TABLE I. Chance expectations and actual performances in a social studies class in relation to *DAT-Verbal Reasoning* scores

DAT Verbal Reasoning Test Score	No. of Pupils	% expected by chance to earn D,E, or F	% actually earning D,E, or F
26–up	19	40	6
18–25	49	40	14
10–17	60	40	36
2–9	63	40	73

Instead of 40 per cent of the highest-scoring pupils being found in the low grades group (as one would expect by chance), only six per cent are found there.[3]

Another example, drawn from the area of industrial testing, is shown in Table II. The *Short Employment Tests (SET)* were administered to 74 stenographers at a single level of job responsibility, and the relationships between scores on the tests and on-the-job proficiency ratings were investigated. The girls were rated as low, average or high in ability; the table shows, for each of these groups, what per cent were in each third on the *Clerical Aptitude* test of the *SET* battery.

By chance alone, the per cent of upper, middle and low scorers in each of the rated groups would be the same – in this case, 33⅓%. The boldface numbers in the table would consist of nine 33's. Note how closely this expected per cent is approximated for those ranked average in proficiency, and for those in the middle third on test score; the percentages in the middle row and those in the middle column run between 28 and 36. Note also that at the extremes – the four corner numbers – the prediction picture is more promising. Among those *rated* low, there are almost three times as many people from the lowest third on the test as there are from

TABLE II. Per cent of stenographers in each third on *SET-Clerical* who earned various proficiency ratings

SET-Clerical Test Score	Proficiency Rating		
	Low	Average	High
Upper Third	18	33	50
Middle Third	29	36	28
Lowest Third	53	31	22
Total Per Cent	100	100	100
No. of Stenographers	17	39	18

the top third. Among those rated high, the per cent from the top third on the test is almost two and one-half times as great as the per cent from the bottom third. The personnel man would do well to be guided by these data in selecting future stenographers, even though the validity coefficient is just .38.

The data in the above examples are based on relatively small numbers of cases (which is typically true of practical test situations) and the per cents found in each category are consequently somewhat unstable. The validity coefficients based on groups of such sizes are, of course, also less stable than coefficients based on large numbers of cases. The wise test user will make several validity studies using successive groups. Having done so, he may take an average of the validity coefficients from these studies as being a more dependable estimate of the validity of the test in his situation. Formal tables are available[4] which can be used to estimate expectancies when the validity coefficient is of a given size and the per cent of successes and failures is known. Table III has been constructed from these formal tables to illustrate the usefulness of coefficients of various magnitudes.

The first part of Table III is based on a failure rate of 20 per cent. It shows the per cent of individuals at different levels on the test who are successful (in marks earned, or dollar sales, or merit rating, or number of widgets assembled, or whatever we are trying to predict) when the validity coefficient is .30, .40, .50, or .60. The columns in boldface at the left show the decile rank on the test – individuals with percentile ranks of 90 to 99 are in the tenth decile or top 10 per cent, those with percentile ranks from 80 to 89 are in the next (9th) decile, etc.; the first decile includes the individuals between the first and ninth percentiles on the test – the 10 per cent who scored lowest. In the first lightface column is shown the per cent of persons in each decile who may be expected to succeed when the validity coefficient (r) is .30; the second column in lightface type

TABLE III. Per cent of successful individuals in each decile on test score —

Standing on the test		when the total per cent of failures is 20%, and				when the total per cent of failures is 30%, and				when the total per cent of failures is 50%, and			
Percentile	Decile	r = .30	r = .40	r = .50	r = .60	r = .30	r = .40	r = .50	r = .60	r = .30	r = .40	r = .50	r = .60
90-99th	10	92%	95%	97%	99%	86%	91%	94%	97%	71%	78%	84%	90%
80-89th	9	89	91	94	97	81	85	89	92	63	68	73	78
70-79th	8	86	89	91	94	78	81	84	88	59	62	65	69
60-69th	7	84	86	88	91	75	77	80	83	55	57	59	61
50-59th	6	82	84	85	87	72	74	75	77	52	52	53	54
40-49th	5	80	81	82	83	70	70	70	71	48	48	47	46
30-39th	4	78	77	77	78	67	66	65	64	45	43	41	39
20-29th	3	75	73	72	71	63	61	59	56	42	38	35	31
10-19th	2	71	68	64	61	59	55	50	45	37	33	28	22
1-9th	1	63	56	49	40	50	43	35	27	29	23	16	10

presents similar expectancy information when $r = .40$, the next column is for $r = .50$, and the last column for a validity coefficient of .60.

What does this table tell us? Suppose that the failure rate among Winsocki College freshmen is about 20 per cent – that usually one out of every five students fails or goes on probation before the end of the year. A selection test is given and a correlation of .30 is found between scores on the test and success in the first year. Ninety-two per cent of those who score in the top 10 per cent of the group on the test may be expected to succeed, while only 63 per cent in the bottom decile can expect to survive the first year. If the validity coefficient is .40, ninety-five per cent in the top decile may be expected to survive; of the lowest scoring students, 56 per cent are likely to be around at the end of the year. The survival rate when $r = .60$ is almost perfect (99 per cent) for the top group; it is only 40 per cent for the lowest scorers.

The last two sections of Table III present similar information for coefficients of .30, .40, .50, and .60 when failure rates are 30 per cent and 50 per cent. The last column at the right shows, for example, that if only 50 per cent of a total group is successful, and the validity coefficient is .60, the top scoring individuals will have a survival rate of 90 per cent; of those in the bottom decile on the test, only one out of ten is likely to succeed.

It is interesting to compare the figures in the column headed $r = .50$ (when failures total 20 per cent) with the quotation with which we began. The "only 13.4 per cent" sort of statement may be (and often has been) misinterpreted as indicating that the test can tell us little. Actually, the test has changed our picture dramatically. Without it, we could say only that for every person the odds are four chances to one he'll succeed. With the test, we can sort the candidates into groups and say that some have distinctly better prospects than others. If three men score, respectively, in the tenth, the seventh and the lowest deciles, we can give odds on their success:

	Without test information	With knowledge of test scores
Man in 10th decile	4 to 1	37 to 1 (97.4%-2.6%)
Man in 7th decile	4 to 1	8 to 1 (88%-12%)
Man in 1st decile	4 to 1	1 to 1 (49%-51%)

What are the practical implications of these facts? Most apparent is the real potential utility of validity coefficients of .60, .50, .40, and even .30; the information they provide is far from useless. For the counselor, they offer increased ability to estimate his client's general chances of success in an educational or vocational pursuit. For the admissions officer in a college, better forecasts of drop-out rate, as well as more informed selection, are possible. For personnel men in industry, data such as these provide information with respect to the selection ratios which will be necessary to obtain a desired number of successful employees.

As do all other statistics, standard errors of estimate and validity coefficients require full understanding. For all of us, our errors of estimate will always be greater than we would like. The precision of our estimates will be less than perfect, and we shall aim constantly to increase that precision. At the same time, if a test will increase appreciably our ability to predict (even though broadly) performance in curricula or careers, let us use it – with caution, but also with gratitude. A blade not sharp enough for shaving can still be used to cut a knot.

References

[1] J. P. Guilford, *Psychometric Methods* (New York: McGraw-Hill, 1936) p. 364. The index of forecasting efficiency $= 100 \ (1 - \sqrt{1 - r^2})$ where r is the validity coefficient, the correlation between the predictor test and the subsequent performance rating or other criterion. When the number of cases is small, a correction term $\left(\dfrac{N-1}{N-2} \right)$ is inserted under the square root sign.

[2] J. P. Guilford, test 304, page 407 in Buros: *The Fourth Mental Measurements Yearbook* (Highland Park, N.J.: The Gryphon Press, 1953).

[3] For semitechnical discussions of everyday ways of demonstrating test validity, see THE PSYCHOLOGICAL CORPORATION'S *Test Service Bulletins* Nos. 37 and 38: "How Effective Are Your Tests?" and "Expectancy Tables: A Way of Interpreting Test Validity."

[4] R. W. B. Jackson and A. J. Phillips, "Prediction Efficiencies by Deciles for Various Degrees of Relationship." *Educational Research Series* No. 11, Dept. of Educational Research, Ontario College of Education, University of Toronto. Especially interested persons may find it worthwhile to see also: H.C. Taylor and J.R. Russell, "The relationship of validity coefficients to practical effectiveness of tests in selection." *Journal of Applied Psychology*, 1939, Vol. 23, pp. 565-578.

Review of the Law School Admission Test

The *Law School Admission Test* is actually a program rather than a test and must be evaluated as such. The most recent form available for review, YLS2, is an outgrowth of earlier forms developed by the testing organization since 1947. At present, the test consists of two booklets which contain six tests. Book 1 consists of a Principles and Cases section (46 items, 45 minutes) in which the applicant judges the relevance of stated principles to the described cases; a Data Interpretation section (35 items, 60 minutes) intended to measure mathematical reasoning; and a Reading Comprehension section (46 items, 60 minutes) containing eight passages with rather general content. Book 2 contains a section called Debates (60 items, 20 minutes) in which the applicant indicates whether a statement supports, refutes, or is irrelevant to the resolution it follows; a Best Arguments section (32 items, 45 minutes) which requires the evaluation of arguments which are offered in described disputes; and a somewhat speeded paragraph reading section (30 items, 10 minutes) in which a word is to be located which spoils the meaning of each of the paragraphs.

No direct estimate of the test-retest reliability of the current form is available. This fact is perhaps not especially surprising since the test is part of a continuous program in which new forms are to be prepared each year. Evidence presented for a previous form (WLS) indicates that it was very reliable. A coefficient of .91 was obtained for a group of 72 applicants who were retested at their own request; since they had been low scorers originally (thus being restricted in range) and claimed illness or other conditions predisposing to an underestimate of their real ability (which would also result in important score changes), the coefficient of .91 may be accepted as probably an absolute minimum of the reliability of Form WLS.

From Buros, Oscar Krisen, Editor, *The Fourth Mental Measurements Yearbook*. Highland Park, N.J.: Gryphon Press, 1953. Pp. 814-816.

It is regrettable that test-retest coefficients have not been presented for the present form since there are some sharp differences in content between the previous and present forms; in a program as extensive as this, into which so much experimental and statistical work has gone, one would expect some opportunities to have arisen for obtaining such reliability estimates. However, the nature of the tests and the data for previous forms would lead to confidence that the present total test scores are unquestionably highly reliable.

Validity studies of the present form must naturally await the completion of a year's academic work by the students. Extensive studies have been reported for Form WLS; a summary reported by Schrader and Olsen presents validity coefficients for 21 groups of students for the *Law School Admission Test* and validity data for prelaw grades, both alone and combined, for 14 of these groups. The 21 LSAT coefficients ranged from .18 to .65; the average r was .44. To the extent that LSAT scores were considered in the admission process, these coefficients are underestimates. Validity coefficients for the prelaw grades alone against average first year law school grades ranged from −.04 to .50; LSAT score and prelaw grades combined yielded coefficients from .34 to .68. The poorest of these coefficients are discouraging (if one forgets the unreliability of the criterion grades and similar considerations); the best of them are heartening. It is a welcome sight to see so many studies reported, and perhaps the variation in success of prediction will indicate to the cooperating law schools how specific validity is. Certainly the differences found from school to school emphasize the inadequacy of tests and programs which cite validity data in only one or two institutions.

The content of the present form seems to have been selected for face validity as well as empirical validity. In keeping with the view set forth by the Policy Committee of the participating law schools, no specific legal information has been included, although an applicant may find it easier to read many of the items if he has previously encountered such legal terms as "warranty," "title certificate," "statutory grant," etc., or is familiar with stilted legal phraseology. The absence of questions on specific information is explained by Schrader and Olsen: "A systematic effort has been made to minimize the role of specific subject-matter preparation in the test and to focus attention on basic abilities. This emphasis should be kept in mind in comparing the validity coefficients (cited above) with those summarized in reviews of other law school tests by Kandel, Adams and Stuit." The reviewer questions that this proposition can stand on its own feet. If it can be demonstrated that an information test does not predict law school grades, or that it adds nothing to a prediction from prelaw grades, then the proposition is acceptable. If, on the other hand, an information test is a valuable member of a predicting team, it has a rightful place in a prediction program which cannot be gainsaid by such a phrase as "basic abilities." The reviewer would prefer empirical demonstrations of ineffectiveness of good general legal information tests to having such tests summarily read out of court.

The instructions sent to supervisors and the attractive pamphlet which each applicant receives are well prepared and contain much useful information. Of particular merit are the provision of a set of sample questions to prepare the student for the kind of examination he will face and a detailed statement informing him of such regulations as apply to the use of slide rules and other devices, the value of a watch for pacing himself, etc. Although the instructions to the student are generally clear and concise, one statement is simply silly. The student is informed that there will be no correction for guessing and advised to use shrewd guesses but to "omit questions about which you have absolutely no knowledge, since you can use your time more profitably in other parts of the test." It is obvious that a student who has necessarily already spent time reading a question can far more profitably immediately record a guess which *might* do him some good and does not penalize him than omit the guess and lose whatever possibilities reside in chance guesses. This admonition may well impair the applicant's confidence in other information given him.

A highly desirable aspect of the program is the preparation of analyses of test results by undergraduate college. This kind of report provides information concerning the caliber of students coming from individual prelaw schools which could not be gathered by most law schools except over a considerable period of time. Activities such as these are potent advantages of a service program over the simple outright purchase of tests. The cost is, of course, much greater, but proper cost accounting of student failure should persuade administrators that having a service program is less expensive than not having one. Another excellent feature is the availability of two parallel forms of the test each year; this is valuable both for security and for retesting if the occasion demands it.

Perhaps just because the organization which runs this program has so much experienced talent available to it, the reviewer takes exception to certain flaws which do not, for the most part, affect the quality of the tests or program as such. For example, reliability coefficients based on odd-even and Kuder-Richardson techniques are reported for tests which are admittedly speeded. This is improper. As another example, a column of validity coefficients is corrected for range on the assumption that each of the schools would have an applicant population as heterogeneous as the total population, and on the further assumption that all such applicants would have been admitted if the tests had not been used to select them. It is doubtful that these assumptions are warranted.

The format of the test booklets is reasonably good and the type face (reduced typewriting) one of the clearer of its species. This last is fortunate, for the size of the type is, in the reviewer's judgment, much too small when it is remembered that the applicant spends several hours reading it. The applicant may not mind very much when there is enough space between the lines, but the longer paragraphs are quite formidable and might well contribute to the reading difficulty of the passages.

In evaluating the program as a whole, certain considerations arise. There seems to be little doubt that the program can contribute to better selection of students in those law schools which do not have their own programs. It seems equally clear that the services performed by the program are real contributions to the cooperating institutions, especially if those institutions do not have skilled measurement people on their staffs. The existence of a program, permitting joint effort and economies, is a good thing. However, are these the best tests for the purpose – the prediction of law school success? We have mentioned above the lack of evidence with regard to the possibilities of an information test. Can validity equal to that now being attained be achieved by more efficient tests in less time, or is four hours really necessary? It would be interesting, for example, to see comparative predictions from the same organization's Verbal Factor and Profile Mathematics sections of the *Graduate Record Examination,* or some similar test of general academic aptitude.

If the separate parts of the *Law School Admission Test* were shown to be differentially predictive of specific law school courses, the length of the present examination could be justified. If the law schools were interested in the broad cultural backgrounds of their applicants, a long multipart test which accomplished that purpose could be justified. That a single-score test with a single purpose needs to be four hours long seems less credible – however, both the law schools and their candidates may believe that a long examination is *ipso facto* a fairer one than a shorter test of equal reliability and validity. Although a number of studies of various item types, some time-consuming and others less so, have been done, one wonders if shorter item types could not be found to compete with the present series.

Reference

SCHRADER, WILLIAM B., AND OLSEN, MARJORIE. *The Law School Admission Test as a Predictor of Law School Grades.* Princeton, N.J.: Educational Testing Service, September 1950. Pp. 10. Paper, lithotyped.

Standardizing an Individual Intelligence Test on Adults: Some Problems

The problems which face the author and publisher who set out to standardize a test on an adult population vary in complexity, intensity, cost, and time consumption according to the nature of the instrument and the rigor of the standards they, the author and publisher, impose on themselves. This paper is concerned with one of the most ambitious attempts of its kind – the standardization of the Wechsler Adult Intelligence Scale. Examples of the problems which have been met are drawn from two projects – from the standardization proper and from a separate study of the aged.

The standardization of WAIS, as the test is usually called, was in many ways unique. The very attempt to obtain a representative sample of the adult population of the United States with an individually administered test was unusual if not unprecedented. What has been achieved represents, it is believed, the best norms that have been collected in this type of situation – although obviously and admittedly they are not perfect. Some of the limitations of the data will become evident in the discussion of the problems which arose.

Before embarking on the standardization testing, two sets of basic decisions had to be made. The first set had to do with defining the population to be sampled. It was necessary to decide:

a. *What age range should be included?* It was agreed after some discussion to test people from 16 to 64 years of age in the following age groups: 16-17, 18-19, 20-24, 25-34, 35-44, 45-54, and 55-64.

b. *What ethnic groups should be included – whites only, or all groups?* The decision was reached not to limit the sample to whites only; whites and non-whites were specified according to their proportions in the national census.

From *Journal of Gerontology*, 1955, *10*, 216-219. Reproduced with the permission of *Journal of Gerontology*.

c. *How many should be tested?* Clearly, the larger the number of cases included, the better for the sample. Equally clearly, the administration of an individual intelligence test to selected subjects is an expensive process; furthermore, the setting of careful controls over the sample to be tested is more important than mere addition of numbers of cases. The controls make it more difficult, and more expensive, to obtain cases, but they give the resulting sample far greater meaning. The numbers finally agreed on were: 200 per age group for the 3 youngest groups, 300 per age decade between 25 and 54, and 200 for the group between 55 and 64, the total being 1700 cases.

The controls to govern the sample to be chosen had next to be decided on. The following controls were finally set forth, each control applying within every age group.

a. *Sex.* An equal number of males and females were to be included.

b. *Education.* Educational level was categorized as: 0 to 8 years of schooling, 9 to 11, high school graduation, 13 to 15 years of education, and college graduation or more advanced study.

c. *Occupation.* Census categories were utilized to form 13 occupational classes, from professional and technical people through clerks and craftsmen, farm laborers and foremen, to students, housewives, and others not in the employed labor force.

d. *Urban-rural.* Communities were classed as rural if they had less than 2500 population and if they were not adjuncts of larger cities.

e. *Geographic region.* Census groupings were used to divide the map of the United States into 4 geographic areas: northeast, north central, south, and west.

These decisions having been reached, the project came up against the first operating problem: how to specify the characteristics of every one of the 1700 individuals to be tested. The U.S. census data for 1950, although vital as a source of information, do not offer tables which embody the several cross-control variables we have imposed. It was not an easy task to prepare charts specifying for each individual his relevant characteristics in such a way as to maintain, as closely as possible, representativeness of the total sample on each of the controls.

When the charts were finally made, it was possible to give each examiner exact specifications for every subject he or she was to locate. For example, one examiner was instructed to test a non-white, rural female, 20 to 24 years of age, engaged in housekeeping in the north central area, and with eighth grade education, or less. Another examiner was asked to test a white male urban proprietor or manager, 35 to 44 years old, with between 9 and 11 years of schooling.

With so many specifications set down for each prospective subject, much time and effort were needed to locate an individual who met all the requirements. But even after an examiner had succeeded in locating a subject who met every specification the subject might refuse to be tested.

Herein lies one of the major operating difficulties involved in standardizing tests on adults rather than children. In standardizing the Wechsler Intelligence Scale for Children it was necessary only to obtain the cooperation of school authorities, who did not have to act as subjects themselves and who were sympathetic with intelligence testing. Once the school's acceptance was had, compliance by children followed; the cases were selected, scheduled, and tested.

The situation was quite different for the adults. The subjects were not always familiar with, or sympathetic with, intelligence testing. Furthermore, since they were themselves to be the persons taking the test, they often seemed to feel threatened by it. As a result, many prospective subjects refused to take the test. Whenever possible, of course, the examiner tried to persuade recalcitrant subjects to relent and comply; sometimes the examiner was successful, sometimes not. When unsuccessful, the examiner then had to seek another prospect who met all the specifications and would agree to be tested.

This matter of willingness of the subject to be tested is of considerable importance even beyond the additional time, expense, and frustration resulting from refusals. A more important consequence is the bias in the representativeness of the sample. It is logical to believe that, on the whole, people who are unwilling to take an intelligence test are less intelligent than their peers who are willing to be examined. A precise estimate of how much bias there is would be difficult, if not impossible, to obtain. That it does exist, and the direction in which it operates, can nonetheless be assumed.

There is another bias which should also be recognized as influencing the sample. This has to do with a kind of cultural selection which is personal to the examiner. It is only natural for an examiner to reach out for subjects from those around him – relatives, friends, and acquaintances. The examiners used in the standardization were all professional people, with above average education. Their friends and acquaintances, it may be expected, were therefore likely to be people who are superior to their own educational and occupational peers. For example, if the writer were asked to test a white craftsman, aged 35 to 44, with 12 years of education, he would draft a carpenter friend who happens to meet these requirements. His friend would be available and compliant; but he would not be representative, in intelligence, of 35 to 44 year old craftsmen with similar education. The writer has found him a congenial companion because he is above average – in knowledge and in intellectual curiosity. It is probable that at least some of the subjects who were most readily available to the examiners were similarly unrepresentative. Again, it is not feasible to compute how much of an effect this congeniality bias has on the sample; it can only be assumed that the bias does exist and operates to increase the raw score required to obtain a given IQ.

The problems noted above (and a number of difficulties not discussed herein) applied to all the age groups in the standardization proper. There were some problems, however, which were particularly troublesome in testing older adults. These may perhaps be best illustrated by reference to a supplementary project, the attempt to extend normative data to older people than those in the regular standardization. Through a grant from the U.S. Public Health Service, the Commission on Human Development of the University of Chicago has been engaged in intensive study of the aged in Kansas City. The cooperation of Dr. Havighurst permitted the tying in of WAIS testing with the larger investigation. The subjects to be tested were the adults aged 60 and over selected by means of an area probability sample drawn from the metropolitan area of Kansas City.

Essentially, the program for obtaining cases was opposite to that used in the main standardization. In the Kansas City study, the subjects were specified in terms of their addresses, and the examiner had to contact the specific examinee, to persuade him or her to participate, and then to administer the test. The problem of *locating* subjects, so troublesome in the standardization proper, was less troublesome in the study of the aged.

This did not mean that the task of the Kansas City examiners was easier than that of examiners in the national study. Although comparative data are lacking, it is reasonably certain that as compared with younger adults, the older potential subjects were, on the average, less familiar with the whole idea of testing and therefore less sympathetic; they were also more likely to be suspicious of the examiner's purposes. The greater age difference between the elderly subjects and the examiners might well have made rapport more difficult. More of the advanced in age were obviously less able physically to make the simple movements involved in the performance portion of the scale; many of these potential subjects nevertheless did the verbal tests and one or more of the performance tests; this is known since their records are available. Quite probably, many other of the physically less able refused to take any part of the scale, once they recognized the kinds of tasks they would be asked to try, although they may have given other reasons for their refusal. Whatever the reason given, it often meant that the subject simply was not tested, despite the continued efforts of one or more of the examiners.

One of the interesting sets of data which were compiled in this study was a record of why prospective subjects were not tested. The examiners, while obtaining complete tests on 352 subjects and less complete tests on 123 more, were unable to test 182. Of those not secured, 90 were men and 92 women. Reasons for failure were classified into 5 categories. One category

– refusal – contained half (90) of the failures; 57 other subjects not secured were either too ill or deceased. The remaining 35 failures were accounted for by such factors as having moved from the city, being unable to understand English, etc.

Some of the subjects' reasons for refusing may be illuminating. The remarks come from report forms filled out for each individual from whom a test was not obtained: A 61 year old housewife contacted by 2 examiners on 5 different occasions said she did not believe in surveys; too many people came to the door; she was just not interested. A 70 year old retired railroad employee, contacted by 3 examiners on 4 occasions said: "If you were selling $10.00 bills for $1.00, I wouldn't be interested." He also remarked, rejecting the examiner's plea, that he was not interested in helping other people. A 64 year old decorator (2 examiners, 3 contacts) said, "I know what you're trying to do. I've been in the selling game too."

The 75 year old wife of the president of a motor company said she did not want to be in the public eye and would hear no explanation; a 61 year old wholesale clothing salesman, learning it was an intelligence test, said he would have no part of it, that he had taken intelligence tests before and knew all the answers; a 67 year old factory operative thought the test was too personal; an 86 year old retired music teacher would say only that she hated everybody except her mother.

There was a woman, described in a special report prepared by one of the examiners as the most paranoid subject encountered, who "ordered the examiner out of the house because of some 'plot' that her sister and the government had contrived against her. Paranoid tendencies were further indicated by the numerous crucifixes hanging from the mailbox, the many crucifixes and religious pictures hanging on the walls, a large faded wreath hanging among the crosses, the furniture swathed in white cloth, the shades pulled down, a heavy mantle of dust coating the interior of the house, and the woman herself wearing numerous strings of rosaries around her neck."

No mention has been made of problems with respect to the conditions under which testing was attempted. Omitted also are problems of test theory and test construction – should time limits be removed, should separate norming techniques be devised, and similar matters of importance and concern. Problems like these nonetheless are real and present, and must be anticipated by anyone who would work in this field.

Perhaps the best advice which can be offered to those who would try similar studies is: be financially prepared for heavy drains on the exchequer; be intellectually prepared to exercise all the ingenuity – your own and your colleagues' – at your command; be emotionally prepared for frustration and the necessity for compromise. Above all, be grateful to the hundreds of men and women who do cooperate with you, to examiners who adapt themselves to working at unusual hours under often difficult conditions as well as to the subjects who, often not even understanding the purpose of your study, give freely of their time and effort to forward your work and contribute to society's knowledge of itself.

Summary

A project aimed at the standardization of an individual intelligence test on a representative sample of adults in the United States – and especially if the research is to include the aged as well as younger adults – must be prepared to cope with problems of:

1. Financial cost – beyond expenditures which are ordinarily possible by an individual.
2. Research facilities – for the production of materials and analysis of the data.
3. Cooperation of competent colleagues to supervise and examine the subjects.
4. Description of a sample of adequate representativeness.
5. Selection of the specific individuals to be tested.
6. Persuasion of the selected individuals to agree to be tested.

If the first three problems cannot clearly be resolved, the project should hardly be undertaken at all; the success with which the last three are met will determine the validity of the norms – the goodness of the job.

Aptitude, Intelligence, and Achievement

Which is more helpful – an aptitude test or an achievement test? – a general mental ability test or a differential aptitude test battery? There are purposes for which each kind of test is superior; there are circumstances in which all are useful; there are conditions when any one of these types may be pressed into service to yield information ordinarily obtained from another type of test. What are these purposes, circumstances and conditions? When should an achievement test be used rather than an intelligence test, or an aptitude test? What advantages do multiple-score aptitude batteries have over single-score intelligence tests?

As a preliminary, let us look at the basic characteristics of achievement tests, intelligence tests and aptitude tests. By definition, an achievement test measures what the examinee has learned. But an intelligence test measures what the examinee has learned. And an aptitude test measures what the examinee has learned. So far, no difference is revealed. Yet three of the traditional categories into which tests are classified are intelligence, aptitude and achievement. Now these categories are very handy; they permit publishers to divide their catalogs into logical segments, and provide textbook authors with convenient chapter headings. Unfortunately, the categories represent so much oversimplification as to cause confusion as to what is being measured. What all three kinds of tests measure is what the subject has learned. The ability to answer a proverbs item is no more a part of the examinee's heredity than is the ability to respond to an item in a mechanical comprehension test or in a social studies test. All are learned behavior.

Moreover, all are intelligent behavior. It takes intelligence to supply the missing number in a number series problem. It also requires intelligence to figure out which pulley will be most efficient, or to remember which

From *Test Service Bulletin* No. 51, The Psychological Corporation, 1956.

president proposed an inter-American doctrine. We can say, then, that an intelligence test measures intelligent behavior, an aptitude test measures intelligent behavior and an achievement test measures intelligent behavior.

Finally, all three types of tests measure probability of future learning or performance, which is what we generally mean when we speak of "aptitude." In business and industry, the chances that an employee will profit from training or will perform new duties capably may be predicted by scores on an intelligence test, by scores on one or more specific aptitude tests, or by some measure of the degree of skill the employee already possesses. Similarly, test users in the schools know that an intelligence test is usually a good instrument for predicting English grades, a social studies test is often helpful for prediction of future grades in social studies, and a mechanical comprehension test is likely to be useful in predicting for scientific or technical courses. So, intelligence tests are aptitude tests, achievement tests are aptitude tests and aptitude tests are aptitude tests.

Content—What the Test Covers

On what basis are the types to be differentiated? One possible basis is that of content. Quite often, we can look at the subject matter of a test and classify the test as achievement or intelligence or aptitude. But content is not a sure guide by any means.

Let us take a specific item. A student is taught to multiply $(x-y)$ by (x). If he demonstrates that he can perform this operation correctly, we accept this item as an achievement measure. Next, without specific formal instruction, he is asked to multiply $(p+q)$ by $(p-q)$, and again answers correctly. Is this achievement? The mathematics teacher would say it is. Is it aptitude? Certainly the ability to perceive the analogy between the taught and untaught algebraic problems is indicative of future learning ability in algebra. Is it intelligence? The demonstrated ability to generalize is clearly symptomatic of intelligence.

The same point can be made with regard to entire subtests. In the *Metropolitan Achievement* series there is a Spelling test; one of the *Differential Aptitude Tests* is also a test called Spelling. Tests of arithmetic comprehension may be found in most achievement batteries; one of the subtests in each of the *Wechsler Intelligence Scales* measures arithmetic comprehension. What does all this mean? Have we demonstrated that the authors of these tests are confused, or is our classification system less neat and simple than it appears to be on the surface?

We believe the classification system is at fault. The teacher who has taught pupils how to solve arithmetic problems is perfectly justified in claiming that the pupils' performance on tests in these abilities represents achievement – both hers and theirs. At the same time, the learning of the skills and appreciations by the pupils is evidence of intelligence.

Furthermore, the possession of the skills and of the ability to learn demonstrates the possession of aptitude for further learning in those same school subjects, and probably in other subjects as well. For example, scores on the *DAT* Spelling Test provide excellent prediction of success in learning stenography.

Process — What the Examinee Has to Do

It would appear, then, that test content is not entirely adequate to discriminate among intelligence, achievement and aptitude testing. Can we use process to discriminate among them? Shall we say that achievement is measured when the subject is tested for recall of what he has been taught, and that intelligence is shown in the ability to generalize from the facts?

Every modern educator and every modern test constructor would reject such classification outright. Rare is the teacher who will admit her students are merely memorizing facts; rare is the curriculum which is not aimed at developing the ability to generalize, to apply learned principles in new situations. Furthermore, inspection of the items in some of our most highly regarded intelligence tests will reveal many items which are as direct questions of fact as any to be found in the least imaginative achievement tests. Processes of recognition, recall and rote repetition may be distinguishable from processes of generalization, appreciation, and problem solving — but apparently they are not satisfactory for distinguishing between intelligence and achievement.

Function—How the Test Results Are Used

If test content will not serve, nor test process, what will successfully discriminate intelligence or aptitude from achievement measures? A logical candidate would seem to be function. What are we trying to accomplish with the test scores? How are the results to be used? What inferences are to be drawn concerning the examinee? If a test's function is to record present or past accomplishment, what is measured may be called achievement. If we wish to make inferences concerning future learning, what is measured is thought of as aptitude. One kind of aptitude test, usually some combination of verbal and numerical and/or abstract reasoning measures, is sometimes called an intelligence test; more properly, in educational settings, it is called a scholastic aptitude test.

In Educational Testing . . .

If the purpose is to evaluate the effectiveness of teaching or training, and the test is designed to measure what has been specifically taught, we have an achievement situation. The more closely the test reflects what has been taught, the better it suits the purpose. The statement holds equally well if the intent is to grade students on the basis of what they have learned in a course. If, in addition, we wish to infer how well a student will learn in the future, we have an aptitude situation. The greater the similarity between what has been learned and what is to be learned, the better the achievement test suits the aptitude purpose. A test of achievement in first term algebra is likely to be an excellent test of aptitude for second term algebra. On the other hand, such a test is likely to predict less well future course grades in physics, French and shop. Nor can an achievement test in algebra be used effectively to predict course grades before the students have been exposed to algebra. Some other measure of aptitude is required.

If we are interested only in predicting algebra grades, a numerical aptitude test is likely to prove best. The chances are, however, that we are also interested in predicting success in other subjects at the same time. In that case, we have several choices. We can select achievement tests in as many relevant or nearly relevant subjects as are available, and use these tests as predictors. This approach will obviously be most effective where past and future courses are most alike; it will be least effective where past and future courses are least alike. Concretely, achievement tests can function as aptitude measures best in the early school years, less well at the junior and senior high school levels where courses become increasingly differentiated.

Another possible choice for predicting success in various courses is the scholastic aptitude or so-called group intelligence test. To the extent that various courses demand verbal and/or numerical facility for successful learning, a test which measures those aptitudes will probably prove useful. Again, this verbal-numerical ability is likely to play a more pervasive role in the elementary grade subjects than in the high school. Even at the high school level, grades are so often affected by the student's verbal expression that scholastic aptitude tests often correlate well with those grades even in subjects such as mechanical drawing and music. In such courses when grades are assigned on the basis of what the student can *do*, rather than how well he can speak or write about it, the predictive value of verbal or verbal-numerical aptitude tests is likely to be less.

A third alternative is the use of differential aptitude test batteries. These batteries ordinarily include measures of verbal and numerical aptitude, just as the scholastic aptitude intelligence tests do; they also provide measures of other aptitudes as well – spatial, mechanical, clerical, and the like. The instruments yield a set of scores which recognize intra-individual differences, accepting the fact that a student may be fairly high in verbal ability, average in numerical, very high in mechanical aptitude, and very poor in clerical speed and accuracy. These multi-score batteries provide broader coverage of mental functioning than is obtainable from the more limited scholastic aptitude test.

Is this broader coverage worth the effort? It depends on what the user wants to accomplish. If only the probability of success in an English class is of interest, a scholastic aptitude test might well suffice – information concerning other abilities may not improve prediction enough to be worth obtaining. If several varied criteria are of interest, as in guidance into an academic, trade or commercial curriculum, the additional information provided by differential aptitude batteries should be well worth the effort. Interest in broad and varied criteria is greatest at the secondary school level, where the pupil reaches points of decision. At this time, the pupil and the school should be considering what kind of curriculum is best for him, what are appropriate directions and levels of aspiration for the immediate and the more distant future. Educational and vocational guidance are of tremendous importance; therefore, the broadest scope of ability testing is both desirable and eminently worthwhile. True, differential aptitude testing takes more time and costs more money. A two-, three-, or four-hour difference in time, or a dollar per pupil difference in cost, should be seen in the perspective of all the years of each student's educational and occupational future. The choices to be made may well set the pattern of the student's life; information to help guide those choices warrants the additional expenditure of minutes and pennies.

And in the Business World

The use of the educational frame of reference should not be taken to mean that the points do not apply to industry. They do. Readers engaged in personnel work in business and industry will have seen parallels between the last few paragraphs and their own problems, but will be conscious of some differences, too. For example, multi-score employment tests are often more useful than single-score tests in employee selection simply because they give a clearer picture of several aspects of ability that are mixed in unknown proportions in the single score. On the other hand, it is more often necessary for the industrial man than for the educator to make do with a less appropriate test. Many of the specific aptitude or achievement tests industry needs simply do not exist as yet, or do not work very well. In such cases, a general mental ability test or a semi-relevant aptitude test may be better than nothing even though we realize that a proficiency test would give us still more useful information about the applicant.

In Summary

Which kinds of tests are most helpful? Any test is helpful or harmful only as it is used properly or misused. The information which can be obtained from group tests of general intelligence, so-called, is often valuable. The information can be misinterpreted, and perhaps the use of the word "intelligence" predisposes somewhat to misinterpretation; but *any* test score can be misinterpreted. The issue is really whether scholastic aptitude or general mental ability tests provide *enough* information, and here one can only say "enough for what?" For some important decisions, and at some educational levels, the information is probably adequate. For other decisions, and at other levels, the additional information provided by differential ability tests is needed.

Whether achievement, intelligence or differential aptitude tests should be used depends on the functions to be served. The test user should ask "what inferences do I want to make; what information do I need to make those inferences?" The user who answers those questions will show intelligence, achievement of proficiency in test usage, and special aptitude for further advances in psychometrics.

The Obligations of the Test User

The conscientious publisher of psychological and educational tests occupies an unusual, if not unique, position. Like the manufacturer of scientific apparatus, he is engaged in the production of instruments to meet the needs of professional people. Like the book publisher, he faces the problems of printing, of editing, of working with authors and their idiosyncrasies, of copyrights. Unlike the manufacturer of scientific apparatus, who can assume that the physicist, chemist or medical doctor understands the apparatus that is purchased, the test publisher can make no similar assumption. And unlike the book publisher, who does not need to concern himself with *who* reads his books (except that it be as many as possible) the test publisher must be constantly and actively concerned with those who use his products, lest those products fall into improper hands.

Further to complicate matters, the ethical publisher, having restricted his market according to the dictates of his conscience, still finds himself with purchasers whose preparation for the use of the published materials varies from complete knowledge and considerable sophistication to little or no training and dismaying naiveté.

The dictates of his conscience are not the only moral force acting on the publisher of educational and psychological tests and techniques. In recent years, much time and thought have been devoted to the consideration of his obligations to the professions and to the general public. Committees on Test Standards have been appointed by the American Psychological Association, the American Educational Research Association and the National Council on Measurements Used in Education for the express purpose of formulating specifications for tests and test manuals. The codes which emerged as a result of their deliberations have been reported by

From *Proceedings of the 1955 Invitational Conference on Testing Problems.* Copyright © 1956 by Educational Testing Service. All rights reserved. Reprinted by permission.

these associations in two pamphlets, copies of which should be in the hands of every test user. They are, on the whole, very sound documents; one hopes that the moral pressure they try to exert will, in the long run, prove beneficial.

Additional pressure is also directed at publishers by Buros' *Mental Measurement Yearbooks,* by test review forms in textbooks such as Cronbach's or Thorndike and Hagen's, and the critical reviews which appear in professional journals. These influences are forces for the good. How effective they really are, is unfortunately a matter for dispute. Just a year or two ago, at one of these ETS Conferences, Oscar Buros offered the exasperated judgment that tests and test manuals published in recent years are not as good as many of those published a quarter of a century earlier. I doubt that many of his colleagues would adopt a similarly extreme position. At the same time, there are those of us who are cynical enough to believe that the mere existence of recommendations and reviews does not *ipso facto* improve the quality of instruments offered to the test user.

Over the years, it is neither the publisher nor the critic who most effectively determines the quality of tests; rather it is the test user. Unless the test user knows what a good test is, and withholds support from those which fail to meet high standards, the recommendations enunciated by organizational committees will be worse than ineffective – they will be put to harmful use as just one more device for deluding the innocent. A statement such as "the author has considered the Technical Recommendations set forth by the APA, AERA, and NCMUE in preparing this manual" could provide an aura of respectability which a given manual may not deserve, and the uncritical might well be misled. There is no Good Housekeeping seal of approval in the field of test publication; there is no substitute for professionally competent and conscientious judgment on the part of the test user. Test publishers have important professional obligations; test users have parallel responsibilities.

Test publishers should refrain from making unsubstantiated claims for the validity of the tests they offer; they should distinguish between what they hope, and what has been demonstrated. Test users should also be able to distinguish between what is hoped and what has been demonstrated; they should reject exaggerated claims of merit despite the attractiveness of the manual's format or the eminence of the author. Validity is a matter of the content of the test and the situation in which it is used. It is not assured by either the renown of the writer or reputation of the package designer.

It is proper and desirable for researchers to try instruments in new applications. One hopes, of course, that in the original selection of tests to be tried, some reasonable hypotheses have guided the researcher in his choice; this is not always the case. In any event, the researcher can make more or less of a contribution by publishing his results. If his results are positive, they serve to alert others of new situations in which a test may be effective; if negative, other researchers may be spared the futile effort of duplicating the experiment.

However, if the user applies a test in a situation for which neither the author nor publisher intended it, a negative result should not be construed as adverse criticism of the test. It may more appropriately be announced as a failure of the researcher's hypotheses to stand up. It is ironic that publishers and authors should so often be blamed when tests won't do what they were never intended to do; when the only fair comment on a study is "why did the researcher *expect* the test to be useful under such conditions?" The publisher may properly be taken to task if his tests don't work when they should; the tests should not be criticized if they don't work in situations for which they were not intended nor recommended.

The summer issue of *Personnel Psychology* contains an example of this abuse. A group of graduate engineers was given a series of tests including *DAT Space Relations, Mechanical Comprehension BB* and *Otis Arithmetic Reasoning*. The authors of the article reporting this research express surprise that the tests failed to discriminate among the engineers. The proper occasion for surprise is that these tests were chosen for use in this situation in the first place! They are good tests for the populations and purposes for which they were intended – high school students or unselected adults. That tests published for these levels do not yield adequate distributions for a group which has had intensive academic and professional experience with mechanical forces and advanced mathematics is hardly noteworthy. If the *Miller Analogies Test*, or the *Minnesota Engineering Analogies Test*, or the *GRE Advanced Mathematics Test* was not discriminative, we might criticize the test; with the tests selected for this study, we can only question the wisdom of the researchers.

Test publishers are constantly engaged in amassing evidence concerning the validity of their instruments in various applications and with different kinds of subjects. Test users must recognize that unless they provide the subjects to be tested, the needed data cannot be accumulated. Few and far-between are the occasions when a test publisher has a captive group of subjects at his mercy. More typically he is wholly dependent on the cooperation of the school administrator, counselor or teacher. The user has the right, and the duty, to refuse to buy a test which lacks proper documentation; he is also under some obligation to accept his proportionate share of the burden of providing a situation in which evidence concerning the test may be gathered during its exploratory, standardization and validation phases. It should not be left to the cooperative minority to provide the necessary subjects; all schools which hope to profit by the existence of good instruments should participate in experimental programs on appropriate tests.

A similar point may be made with respect to already existing tests. The publisher who neglects to collect serviceable normative data for his tests is properly to be criticized. Is less criticism due the non-cooperators in the schools – and in industry, government and private practice – who have useful normative data in their files but do not make those data available to the publisher and, through him, to their colleagues? How many millions of test scores repose in dusty files, or have been destroyed, which could have augmented the norms in the hundreds of manuals now in print?

Publishers should not over-emphasize the role which their tests should play in the over-all evaluation of a student, employee or client. The user might well apply an equal sense of perspective. It is difficult to say which has done the testing movement more harm – the naive optimist or the equally naive pessimist. The optimist looks to tests to solve all his evaluation problems – in effect, he surrenders the responsibility of personal judgment in exchange for the luxury of having something else make his decisions; often, it is a "something else" which was uncritically chosen in the first place. He operates as a clerk rather than as a professional man.

The naive pessimist, on the other hand, casts his jaundiced eye on the acknowledged limitations inherent in even the best of our tests. Though he would probably not say so boldly, he rejects the tests, in effect, because they don't have perfect reliability or perfect validity. If, in spite of his protestation, tests are used in his school, he warns in doleful tones that the scores must not be used alone as a basis for evaluating the individual.

We have no quarrel with the principle that a single test score – or for that matter, a series of test scores – should not provide the sole basis for action of any kind. Publishers typically urge users to correlate the information obtained from tests with all other relevant information that can be obtained, including grades in school, anecdotal records, physical reports, social workers' reports and whatever else local facilities permit. Our quarrel is that the naive pessimist wears blinders.

It is true that tests are not perfectly reliable or valid; is perfect reliability or validity to be found in grades? in anecdotes? in teacher observations? It is likewise true that tests alone are insufficient evidence for total evaluation of the student. Are we, however, to be satisfied with the evidence we obtain from grades alone? from anecdotes alone? from social workers' visits alone? One wonders whether it is not a sincere compliment (though perhaps unintended) that tests are singled out for warning with regard to their use in isolation; could it be that test scores are the only kind of information which would be considered tempting enough for such use? Nothing is that good, of course – but it is interesting that no one ever warns us about the isolated use of anecdotes or teacher observations.

The publisher has the obligation of keeping abreast of new developments in educational and psychological principles and practice, and of building tests which will reflect those modern concepts. The user is equally obligated to understand these newer instruments and the ideas they represent. We are sometimes told by administrators that, while they approve of intelligence measures with differential scores, such instruments can't be used because their teachers (or counselors) are used to the simple, single IQ. Is this reasonable? These same teachers are expected to look at a cumulative record showing grades in a variety of subjects and extract meaningful information. Multi-score achievement batteries are the rule, almost without exception; yet the teachers have presumably learned to interpret results from these tests. Why, then, should teachers and counselors be accused of inability to learn to interpret several scores on differential aptitude or intelligence tests? The logical answer seems to be that they can learn – if the administration takes its own responsibility seriously enough to provide the opportunity and motivation for learning. Modern medicine requires the general practitioner to understand the properties of modern wonder drugs. Modern education requires modern testing embodying modern concepts – and a willingness on the part of educators to continue their own education.

The preparation of a manual which provides the necessary instructions for administration, scoring and interpretation is an obvious duty of the publisher. Following those instructions is a parallel responsibility of the user. Every one of us, I dare say, has seen impossible scores reported on answer sheets, in personnel files or on cumulative record cards. I recall, for example, a set of records from a New York City school which contained half a dozen or so IQs of 400 and over, twice that many in the 300's and as for IQs of 200 or so, they were quite routine. I recall also a high school testing in Nebraska in which all but three or four of the seniors scored above the ninety-fifth percentile (national norms) on a clerical speed test. As my daughter would say, "Somebody goofed!"

One hopes that no responsible person gave serious credence to such outlandish scores, though their presence in official records does make one wonder. More serious than these dramatic bits of nonsense are the thousands of less dramatic, and consequently less conspicuous, scores which seem possible enough but which are really incorrect reflections of the testee's ability – misleading information as a result of someone's failure to read and heed test manuals.

The list of users' responsibilities could be expanded almost indefinitely; the points selected above are illustrative rather than exhaustive. The whole matter can perhaps best be summarized in two sentences. The publisher should feel obligated to prepare instruments which earn the user's respect by being psychometrically sound, conceptually modern, and administratively and economically practical. The user is under an even stronger obligation to cooperate in the development of these instruments and to support those which deserve support – not only in terms of purchase but also in terms of intelligent application and interpretation. The best portrait painter in the world would be handicapped by a house-painter's four-inch brush; the finest artist's brush obtainable would create no masterpiece in the hands of the untutored.

A Test Battery for Teaching Tests and Measurements

Teachers of measurement courses, or of units on measurement in other courses, are constantly faced with a need for illustrative materials. When students are learning what tests are about, there is no substitute for experience in taking tests. However, the furnishing of actual test copies to students poses practical and ethical problems for the psychologist and educator. The latter considerations are made evident in the code adopted by the American Psychological Association in 1954 under the title "Ethical Standards of Psychologists." The following principles are quoted from that code.

> Principle 5.42-2. Good professional practice demands that test materials be retained by students only if they are graduate students in fields in which tests are professional equipment, and if they have the professional maturity which suggests that they will use tests properly and protect them from abuse by others.
>
> Principle 5.42-3. Instructors of courses which require the taking or the administration of tests by students for didactic purposes should protect the examinees by ensuring that the tests and test results are used in a professional manner, and should make adequate provision for the counseling of any student disturbed by the testing procedure.
>
> Principle 5.47-1. Instructors are expected to manage the use of psychological tests and other devices, the use of which might be spoiled by familiarizing the general public with their specific contents or underlying principles, in such a way as to limit access to them to persons who have a professional interest and who will safeguard their use.
>
> (1) Demonstrations of tests and related devices to non-professionals, whether students or general public, should be planned to illustrate the nature

Reprinted from *13th Yearbook*, 1956, copyright by the National Council on Measurement in Education, East Lansing, Michigan.

of the device (if this can be done without spoiling the test itself), but should avoid incidental or specific coaching in the use of the actual materials of the test or device.

The injunctions imposed on the measurement teacher by these rules of conduct must be treated seriously; few of us would lightly ignore ethical standards set forth for the protection of the community and the profession. At the same time, it is clear that compliance with these restrictions deprives us of one of our most effective teaching methods.

The practical problems of providing students with experience in test-taking and test administration are equally troublesome. If the experience is to be varied enough to permit real learning to occur, it should embrace several types of tests. For the graduate student majoring in tests and measurements, the amount of class time required to take six or eight different kinds of tests may be justifiable. For any other students, the instructor can ill afford to devote a minimum of three or four class meetings to having the students sit and take tests. The conscientious teacher of a class in tests and measurements has too much material that must be covered to permit himself such scheduling. As for the teachers of other courses, in which tests and measurements represent but one topic, such test-taking time is simply out of the question entirely.

The Psychological Corporation has now prepared at least a partial solution to this two-headed problem. Tests should not be placed in the hands of students because to do so endangers the test for other uses, and because of inherent dangers of misinterpretation of scores. A set of tests is now available which has no uses other than instructional; its scores are not likely to be misinterpreted because they are not intended for interpretation in the usual ways of educational and psychological test scores. There are practically no norms provided, nor are there claims that good performance (i.e., getting a lot of right answers) is predictive of anything.

As for time requirements, even the teacher of an incidental unit on measurement may find relief. The ten tests in this battery have a total working time of thirty-five minutes; even if we include time for directions and for distributing booklets, the entire set of ten different tests can be given in less than one hour.

The *Multi-Aptitude Test*, as this unique battery is named, was prepared by E. E. and L. W. Cureton of the University of Tennessee, with the collaboration of a number of their advanced graduate students. Some of its virtues are paradoxical, since they would be defects if found in other instruments. We have already mentioned the absence of claims that the tests will be predictive, and reported the absence of any meaningful norms. Additional virtues are the lack of uniformity of scoring keys, item forms and scoring formulas.

In preparing other test batteries, the authors and publisher strive to use as few item forms, as few kinds of scoring keys and as few scoring formulas as possible. The *Multi-Aptitude Test* uses a punched-hole stencil, a window-type stencil, a fan key and a strip key. In taking the complete battery, the student fills in blanks as he would on an IBM answer sheet, marks a cross in one of four boxes, writes answers to arithmetic problems, and prints words or letters in boxes or other answer spaces. Scoring formulas include Rights only, Rights minus Wrongs, Rights minus one-half Wrongs, and Rights minus one-third Wrongs.

In some batteries, these mechanical arrangements would be unforgivable; for the *Multi-Aptitude Test* this lack of uniformity was planned. It is intended to provide the student with exposure to a variety of experiences in a very short period of time. In addition to meeting all kinds of directions, he encounters test content in Vocabulary, General Information, Arithmetic, Number Series, Figure Classification, Mechanical Comprehension, Word Recognition, Scrambled Letters, Checking, and Paper Form Board. This, we believe, is as much content as most students are willing to experience in just thirty-five minutes of working time.

Specific uses for the battery will have already occurred to you. However, permit me to report some of the authors' suggestions:

1. Instructors of any college courses in psychology or related areas where tests and their uses are discussed may hand out to the students copies of the *Multi-Aptitude Test* for illustration of test content, and may administer all or parts of it.

2. Psychologists and educators often address civic groups or attend conferences held by laymen having a legitimate interest in tests and their effective employment. The *Multi-Aptitude Test* may be distributed to such persons to depict points which otherwise might call for either extended or unsatisfactory verbal description.

3. Students in elementary courses in psychological and educational measurement need to take, administer, score, and interpret a fair variety of typical aptitude tests. In such courses, time is limited: the class time available for students to take and study such tests; the time of the groups to which students administer tests for practice; and the time during which students can learn by doing the actual scoring. The instructor or student can administer one form of the *Multi-Aptitude Test,* with its ten subtests, in one standard 50-minute period. One subtest can be administered by a student for practice to his own or some other class, at a cost in class time of only eight to twelve minutes. The data yielded by one administration of the test to a small class will usually be sufficient to illustrate a variety of test profiles.

4. Courses in psychological and educational statistics are likely to be more interesting and effective if the students use real data for their practice problems. Administration of the *Multi-Aptitude Test* to a group of moderate size will provide data for ten frequency distributions and 45 correlations.

5. For advanced courses in test construction, theory of measurement, and the like, the *Multi-Aptitude Test* also may be used as a source of original data. Since the test has two parallel forms, they may be administered to some suitable group at two different class periods, preferably about a week apart. Then the data can be used to exemplify practice effects, parallel-form test reliability, and even the procedures of factor analysis.

Additional ways of utilizing these tests will be recognized by every instructor; the suggestions mentioned above are merely suggestive of the broad areas in which these materials can make a contribution. Basically, what we offer is ten tests which may be given in a very short period of time, with variety of subject matter, item-response methods, scoring keys and scoring formulas. Each teacher will decide for himself how he can best profit by the availability of the battery.

The tests will not be recommended for any but teaching purposes. Industrial or government agencies seeking to purchase them will be warned that these tests are uncontrolled with respect to purchaser, and that their use for selection or classification purposes would therefore be ill-advised. Teachers of tests and measurements, however, should find this series made to order for them — for it was!

Comparability vs. Equivalence
of Test Scores

The vagaries of the English language must be a source of considerable bewilderment to those who are faced suddenly with the need to learn our tongue. How does one learn what "fix" means? The mariner who wishes to determine his position gets a fix; the professional crook seeks a game that he can fix; the squeaky door needs to be fixed; a committee chairman fixes a date; a student eyes his professor with a fixed stare; a culprit is found and blame is fixed – and the culprit finds himself in a fix. So, too, the special language of tests and measurements contains some ambiguities. But lest they interfere with clear understanding of important concepts, ambiguities ought to be clarified. Two of the common words in the testing field which are surrounded by confusion are "comparable" and "equivalent."

Two test scores are *equivalent* if either can properly be substituted for the other. Both the trait being measured and the means of measurement must correspond. Two scores may be *comparable*, on the other hand, yet reflect very dissimilar abilities. In fact, the scores may be numerically quite different – may even be expressed in different units – and still be comparable.

Comparability properly refers merely to rank in a group; the term carries no connotation with respect to what is being measured. For example, within the *Differential Aptitude Tests* a score of 56 on the Clerical Speed and Accuracy test is comparable for certain individuals to a score of 47 on the Mechanical Reasoning test. In each case, the score represents the 70th percentile for tenth grade boys in the population used in standardizing the tests. The central fact to be noted is that *two scores are comparable if they represent the same standing in the same population.* There is no implication that the scores denote the same, or even similar, abilities. Even casual inspection of the two tests reveals how little they measure in common. In

From *Test Service Bulletin* No. 53, The Psychological Corporation, 1958.

fact, the average correlation between the Mechanical and Clerical tests is about .10.

If a low coefficient of correlation between two sets of test scores doesn't preclude comparability, neither does a high one, assure it. As indicated above, the size of the correlation coefficient is irrelevant to the matter of comparability. Scores on the *DAT* Numerical Ability test and the *Stanford* Arithmetic test are not comparable even though these two tests may be expected to correlate about .75. Scores on these tests are not comparable because the tests were not standardized on the same population. For similar reasons, scores on the *DAT* Space Relations test are not comparable to scores on the *Revised Minnesota Paper Form Board,* although both are tests of space perception. It is not what the tests measure but the population used in standardizing the tests that determines comparability.

But, we may ask, if comparability is merely a matter of giving two tests to one population, cannot one make *any* two tests comparable by giving them to a single group? Yes, indeed. Any school or business organization *can* develop sets of comparable scores by giving any two (or more) tests to its students or employees.

Will such data then be useful to other institutions? That depends on the resemblance between the group on which comparability of scores was based, and the group with which the result is to be used. If the groups are sufficiently alike, a table of comparable scores will apply about as well to the second as it does to the first group. If, on the other hand, the two groups are unlike in some important respect (e.g., age, sex, education, relevant environment, etc.), it may be inadvisable to assume that the table of comparable scores will apply as well to the second group. For example, among tenth grade boys a score of 44 on the *DAT* Mechanical Reasoning test is comparable to a score of 34 on the *DAT* Sentences test; both are at the sixtieth percentile for this norms group. Among tenth grade girls, the same Mechanical Reasoning score of 44 is comparable to a Sentences score of 66; both are at the ninety-fifth percentile for girls in the tenth grade. Like norms and validity, comparability is specific to the group on which the data are obtained.

It may seem surprising that two scores which represent equal standing in one group may reflect quite different standings in another group. Some thoughtful consideration, however, will make it evident that such variations in comparability should be expected. An example may help to illuminate the issue. Let us suppose that a test of English grammar and a test of reading comprehension in French have been administered to two groups of students. Group A consists of freshmen who have had only three months of exposure to the learning of French; Group B consists of sophomores who have just completed two years of course work in the subject. We now prepare distributions of scores for the pair of tests and then compute percentiles to show what per cent of students fall below each score on each test. We compute these percentiles separately for the freshmen and sophomores. For the freshmen, we find the score at the 50th percentile on the English grammar test, and the score at the 50th percentile on the French reading comprehension test. These two scores are comparable – *for the freshmen*. What happens when we seek similarly comparable scores for the sophomores? On the English grammar test the score which is at the 50th percentile for sophomores is likely to be a little higher than the median for freshmen. The French comprehension score at the 50th percentile for sophomores is likely to be very much higher than the score at the 50th percentile for freshmen. The increased knowledge of French represented by the additional year and two-thirds of study will have a greater effect on the French test scores than an additional year of exposure to English. We may expect, then, that the French score comparable to a particular score in English will be appreciably higher for sophomores than for freshmen.

Table I has been prepared to illustrate the situation. Inspection of the table shows that, for freshmen who have studied French for three months, an English grammar score of 58 is comparable to a French comprehension score of 64. For sophomores who have finished two years of French, however, an English grammar score of 58 is comparable to a French comprehension score of 73 – a substantial difference. Clearly, any attempt to apply these freshman data on comparability to the sophomores would result in serious error. Proper interpretation of comparable scores requires that we know the characteristics of the group on which comparability was established. If we wish to apply published tables of comparable scores to our local population, we need to assure ourselves that the groups are sufficiently similar to permit such generalization.

Perhaps the most important distinction between "comparability" and "equivalence" is that, *whereas test content is irrelevant to comparability, test content is fundamental to equivalence.* Two test scores are equivalent if they can properly be substituted for one another. Essentially, this means that scores from one test must represent the same psychological or educational qualities in the individual as do scores from the other test. Most precisely, two tests are completely equivalent if their content is essentially identical and they measure with equal precision (reliability). If these conditions are met, it does not matter which of the two tests is used. These conditions are ordinarily most closely approximated where parallel forms of a test have been constructed – forms which are intended to be interchangeable.

When parallel forms of a test are available, there is ordinarily the implicit, if not explicit, assumption that these forms *are* actually interchangeable. This means that we have no basis for suggesting that a person

TABLE I. Illustrative Norms for Two Groups

Percentile	Freshmen		Sophomores	
	English Grammar	French Reading	English Grammar	French Reading
99	82	88	82	98
97	78	85	79	95
95	75	82	76	92
90	72	79	74	89
85	70	77	72	86
80	68	75	70	84
75	67	73	68	83
70	65	72	67	81
65	64	70	66	80
60	63	69	64	79
55	62	68	63	78
50	61	67	62	76
45	59	66	61	75
40	58	64	60	74
35	57	63	58	73
30	56	62	57	72
25	55	60	56	70
20	53	59	54	68
15	51	57	52	66
10	49	54	50	64
5	46	51	47	61
3	44	48	45	58
1	40	44	42	54

This table is but slightly adapted from tables of norms found in the published manuals for a test of English grammar and a test of French reading comprehension. The scores are standard scores based on a single scale, with a standard deviation of approximately 10.

take one form rather than another – the information obtained will be of equal value whether Form A or Form B is administered. The specific items in one form are of no greater significance than the items which happen to be in the alternate form.

Assumptions we can make with regard to content and reliability of parallel forms of one test are not readily acceptable when we are dealing with two somewhat different tests of the same general ability. This situation is one in which the problem of equivalence frequently arises. For example, a counselor may have reading comprehension scores from the *Stanford Achievement Test* for some pupils, and scores from the *Iowa Silent Reading Test* for other pupils; or, an industrial organization may wish to substitute a modern clerical aptitude test for an outmoded one. In such cases, it is important to know the degree of equivalence of the scores from the two reading tests, or the two clerical tests.

In these circumstances, the size of the coefficient of correlation between the tests is of prime importance. Obviously, lack of perfect reliability in each of the tests will prevent the correlation coefficient from reaching 1.00. Even disregarding the effects of unreliability, however, the correlation would still be less than perfect because each reading test was constructed somewhat differently from the other; the two clerical tests were also prepared according to distinctly different plans. The greater the divergence in specific abilities measured, the more ambiguous the term "equivalent" becomes.

If the correlation coefficient is 1.00, we can say with complete confidence that all persons who score in, say, the sixth decile (51st to 60th percentiles) on one test will also score in the sixth decile on the other. If the coefficient is .90, we may expect that, of those who score in the sixth decile on one test, 22.5% will score in the sixth decile on the other test; the remaining 77.5% will be distributed as follows: approximately 20% each in the fifth and seventh deciles, about 13% in the fourth and eighth deciles, and the remainder in the second, third, ninth, and tenth deciles. If the coefficient is .75, of those who score in the sixth decile on the first test, we may expect 15.2% to score in the sixth decile on the second test. The other examinees would be found in the first decile (1.9%), the second decile (6.0%), the third (9.6%), the fourth (12.4%), the fifth (14.2%), the seventh (14.6%), the eighth (12.9%), the ninth (9.4%), and the tenth decile (3.8%). In these circumstances, we cannot say that an individual will certainly achieve the same score on one test as he does on another. Instead, we can speak only of the *probability* that people who make a certain score on one test will obtain various scores on the other.[1]

In practice it would be extremely awkward to present a table of equivalents in terms of these probabilities. To simplify matters, we present pairs of individual scores as equivalents – usually based on the equi-percentile method or a variant of it. That is, we find for a given group those scores which are at the 40th percentile on Forms A and B, and present those scores as equivalent. What distinguishes the procedure from that in

---

[1]The above statements apply to alternate forms of tests as well as to tests intended to measure somewhat different abilities. If alternate forms of a test correlate .75, the per cents to be expected in each decile will be the same as for a coefficient of .75 between non-parallel tests.

which we obtain comparability of scores is that we have in the equivalence table the assumption that what is being measured is the same in the two forms.

Does this mean that an older test cannot be replaced by a newer and presumably better test? Not at all. To persist in the use of instruments when more valid or more efficient tests become available is poor practice. The heart of any test use is validity – whether the test is doing what it is intended to do. If test N can offer appreciably better prediction than test Q, test N should replace test Q in the particular situation; in this case we do not want a truly equivalent test – we want a better test. If we have had a good deal of experience with test Q, we may wish to know the relative rank represented by specific scores on tests Q and N. If we have used a cutoff score on test Q, we may wish to know what score on test N would eliminate a similar proportion of the applicants. This information can be obtained by giving both tests to the same population, or to two very similar populations.

The resulting table of matched scores is a table of comparability. To evaluate the degree to which the table is also a table of equivalents, we need to know the coefficient of correlation between the two sets of scores. If the scores are comparable and we use the same cutoff score on test N that we used for test Q, we will accept the same number of applicants. Because the tests are not perfectly reliable nor precisely equivalent, we will not accept precisely the same individuals by means of the two tests – and because test N is more valid, we will accept a larger number of good applicants and a smaller number of prospective failures. This is an outcome much to be desired. We are obviously not seeking precise equivalence. We are happy to trade some precision in the equivalence for some improvement in validity.

To summarize, comparable scores represent equal rank in a given population – they imply nothing concerning what is being measured. Equivalent scores represent similarity of what is being measured – the more complete the equivalence, the greater the likeness of measurement. The test user would do well to keep these distinctions in mind; to avoid being confused into accepting comparable scores as denoting equivalence of measurement; to insist on close approximations to complete equivalence in alternate forms; and to recognize that in substituting one test for another he may prefer rough equivalence to more precise equivalence if he is seeking to improve validity.

What Kinds of Tests for College Admission and Scholarship Programs?

The tests we need for college admissions purposes are those which are reliable, efficient, inexpensive, confidential, comprehensive, unique, reflective of the curriculum, independent of the curriculum, fair to late developers, and valid for every curriculum in every institution of higher learning. Unfortunately, no such set of tests exists. In fact, no such set of tests can exist. The demands of each institution are, or should be, unique – the tests one college needs will necessarily differ in some ways from the tests other institutions need. Any attempt to specify the same testing program for all colleges, or all scholarship purposes, is inherently self-defeating.

The central issue in choosing tests for college admissions purposes is the same as for any other purposes – what use is to be made of the test results? This in turn depends on the nature of the individual institution – its goals, its role in our society, its facilities, its philosophy. The growing prevalence of national and statewide programs embodies a real danger that individual differences among institutions of higher education will be overlooked. The advantages of uniform testing programs may be purchased at the excessive price of ignoring one of the greatest strengths of our educational system – the variety of functions performed by our colleges and universities. If every institution were concerned with selecting for admission only the intellectually elite and in providing the same kind of education to all those it admitted, a single set of tests might be prescribed for all. As long as we have state universities and highly selective private colleges, liberal arts colleges and agricultural colleges, cultural emphases and vocational emphases, it is unlikely that one set of tests, or one program of tests however thoughtfully devised, will adequately serve the needs of all. Rather a variety of tests and a variety of programs is essential if each institution is to approximate the requirements of its own special circumstances.

Certainly every institution needs tests which are reliable; but is the same test reliable for every institution? Not unless it is a most inefficient instrument. Our institutions of higher education vary widely with respect to the levels of talent in the students they admit. If a test is to have enough difficult material to discriminate reliably among the top twenty per cent of our students, and enough easy material to discriminate reliably among the bottom twenty per cent of college freshmen, the test will be far too long for practical use in either group. Further, the large number of easy items is likely to bore the better students almost as much as the large number of difficult items frustrates the less able; and, in each case, the sections of inappropriate difficulty represent inefficient measurement.

An example may focus the problem of range of talent more sharply. In one state university system last year, the same set of tests was used in all the units of the system. The average verbal test score of the entering freshmen in one of the institutions (College A) was more than two standard deviations below the average score of those entering another institution (College B) in the same system. College B, whose freshmen scored highest in the state system, was only average among all the schools which use this test. This suggests that differences in mean scores between the most selective schools using this test and low-scoring College A are fully four to five standard deviations. It is probable that for a majority of the students in College A the later half of the test provided a depressing experience, but no real measurement. For these examinees the effective portion of the test was composed of perhaps half the items printed in the booklet. The reliability of the test for discriminating among these students must be assumed to have suffered accordingly.

The tests should be efficient – they should occupy as little of the school's and the student's time as is necessary. This is not to say that the time spent in testing is not as well spent as if equal time were devoted to other kinds of experience to which a student might be exposed. Rather, it suggests that efficient tests permit the gathering of more information within reasonable time limits. If four hours are to be devoted to testing, we should seek full value for those four hours. There are programs which compel some students to stay overnight in an out-of-town lodging; if more efficient testing can eliminate this burden, such programs should be made more efficient. The student may not be in a position to protest;.but the captive state of the student should not make his captors less merciful.

To be most effective, tests should supplement information which is otherwise available, rather than duplicate such information. The college which draws its students from a small number of local secondary schools should be able to accept the students' high school records as evidence of their academic preparation; achievement tests are of secondary utility if they are devoted to assessing the same information as is represented by well-understood school grades. Where there is considerable diversity among feeder schools in their curricula and grading standards, the use of achievement tests may be more defensible. However, in our enthusiasm for tests we should not forget what research has so often demonstrated – that even where students are drawn from diverse secondary schools, high school average is often one of the best predictors of performance in college. Accordingly, instruments which are less directly reflections of the subject matter competence of the student may provide more new information concerning him than do tests in subject matter for which grades are already available.

There are at least two other advantages to the use of non-curricular tests. The use of achievement tests for college admissions all too often exerts a disproportionate influence on the secondary school curriculum and the secondary school teacher. Achievement tests are valid if they measure what the school wants to teach; but schools frequently behave as though their teaching is valid if their students do well on some esteemed achievement test. Some years ago it was commonplace in New York to hear the complaint that the final semester of a course was devoted entirely to specific preparation of the students for the Regents examination; then, for several years, the issue appeared to have been resolved. Today, once again, another set of tests occupies a similarly dominant position. Those of us who are responsible for developing such tests may find ready refuge in the statement that *we* do not recommend that the school or teacher adopt this subservient role – that the tests are intended to follow, not determine, the curriculum. But as long as subject matter tests serve college admissions purposes, we must expect teachers who are anxious to help college-bound students – and teachers whose own performance will be judged by their pupils' success on these tests – to concentrate on the tests as much as on the course.

A second advantage of tests which are not curriculum oriented is their potential for rescue functions. There are students whose formal academic preparation is defective – those who were unstimulated by their courses or their teachers – who may nevertheless be salvaged. Their previous failure to learn may have been the result of delayed maturity on their part, or of an uninspired educational environment. That these students have *not* learned what their courses offered would be documented by course grades and by achievement tests alike. To reveal that they *could* learn requires a different kind of predictive measure.

The proportion of students who do poorly in high school, then find themselves when they are given a chance to do college work, may be small, but the absolute number of such students is large enough to warrant serious attention. A large midwestern state university found in its 1957 entering class 188 students who scored among the top twenty-five per cent on the *College Qualification Tests*, and were in the lowest quarter of their high school class. More than half of these students attained a first semester grade point average of 2.0 (C) or better. In this same class, there were 314 freshmen who were also in the top quarter on the CQT and in the third quarter in high school rank. Three-fourths of these freshmen earned a grade point average of 2.0 or better. These are students – 300 of them in a single freshman class – for whom prognosis on the basis of past academic achievement would be pessimistic, but who were correctly identified by the tests as being capable of at least initially satisfactory work in college.

There are a number of considerations which each institution must resolve for itself before it adopts an admissions battery or accepts a program devised by some outside agency.

1. Will a policy of selective admissions be practiced, or is the institution obliged, perhaps by state charter, to admit all applicants who meet certain minimum requirements?

A highly esteemed private liberal arts college has the privilege of selecting only those students who show greatest intellectual promise. Some state universities do not have that same privilege. Society has prescribed that not only the elite shall be educated; all who can profit from collegiate education in diverse curricula and at varying levels of intellectual demand are to be given the opportunity for further academic training. It is true that even publicly supported institutions are finding it necessary, because of swelling hordes of applicants and limited classroom capacities, to exercise some selection. But the exclusion of the least promising from the great mass of applicants is a quite different task from that of choosing a small number of the elite from an already self-selected group of top-ranking candidates. One should expect that tests differing in difficulty, and perhaps in kind, are necessary for these different tasks.

2. Whether or not selective admissions will be practiced, are students placed in different classes or sections on the basis of test results?

If freshman courses are offered at more than one level to students with different academic preparation, achievement tests may be useful to appraise the student's competence at entrance. If there is a course in chemistry for advanced students and another for students who have not previously taken chemistry – and *if* the student's record of high school courses is judged insufficient to testify to his knowledge of the subject – a chemistry test may be advisable. If, on the other hand, the same first course is offered to all students regardless of previous exposure, a subject matter test is probably less crucial.

3. Will the faculty make use of the test results in its teaching, or are the tests primarily to serve a screening function?

If the biology or history teacher will use the information gained from tests in his subject matter to plan his instruction, achievement tests may be desirable for students entering the course. There is many a faculty member who, rightly or wrongly, expresses indifference to how much subject matter the student has learned before he enters the class; rather, it is whether the student can learn, and is willing to learn, what the professor wishes to teach him that is crucial. This teacher may be one who is unconvinced by the suggestion that what the student has learned in the past is predictive of what the student will learn in the future. Or, this may be a teacher who, faced by overflowing classes of students with a wide range of previous preparation in the subject, has recognized the futility of trying to tailor his teaching to the varying amounts of knowledge possessed by the individual entering freshmen. All students are treated by these two professors as essentially equal and uninformed on entrance to the class. High school course records in the subject are not seen as helpful by these professors; achievement test results are likely to be equally ignored by them.

If a test is to be used primarily as a screening device rather than as a basis for instruction, a scholastic aptitude measure will be more efficient and more broadly applicable than a subject matter test.

4. How many curricula does the school offer?

The small liberal arts college may require that all students take a standard, prescribed curriculum for the most part, with a small number of electives. A large state university may be composed of a number of colleges – such as science and letters, agriculture, education, nursing, pharmacy and engineering – with each college in turn offering more than one curriculum. The variety of curricula in the state university probably assures that the student bodies of the several colleges also vary, in level of ability as well as in areas of academic interest. A minimal program which would prove satisfactory for the homogeneous freshman class of the liberal arts college might well prove inadequate for the heterogeneous population which enters the complex state university.

Dr. Harold Gulliksen, discussing several papers at a recent symposium said, in effect, "Once again we have heard excellent presentations of the problems in this area and the questions that need to be asked. It would be nice if, sometime, we might have a paper which supplied answers." Since the views embodied above express the conviction that no single battery of tests will serve equally in all institutions, an attempt to propose such a battery would be inconsistent. Nonetheless, a general approach can be presented.

The core of an admissions testing program should include measures which appraise the student's command of our two most important symbol systems, verbal and quantitative. The ability to manipulate verbal and numerical concepts has almost invariably been shown to be associated with success in future learning at all educational levels. Opinions differ as to how these abilities may best be tapped – by synonyms, antonyms or verbal analogies, by number series, problem-solving, or numerical computation – but there should be little dispute that some kind of effective appraisal of verbal and numerical abilities is essential. A third component might be a brief test of information, sampling broadly from the general areas of physical and social science. This test would be intended to provide some reflection of the student's educational background where feeder schools and their marking systems are diverse. As a fourth component, a reading test might well be included as much for use in guidance and identification of students in need of remedial training as for predictive purposes. Then, because the student's outlook toward school may indicate how he will react to the educational process, a survey of his beliefs and attitudes with respect to study, to teachers and to the general academic environment might well be in order. Beyond this core, additional testing with respect to special abilities (such as space perception) or specific subject matter competence (e.g., formal mathematics), may ·be added according to the particular character of the institution and the readiness of faculty to utilize the test results as a basis for teaching.

With respect to tests as a basis for awarding scholarships, one needs first to inquire what purpose the scholarships are to serve. If we are simply seeking the academically most promising, then a verbal and numerical test of sufficient difficulty to challenge the top two, or five, or ten per cent of secondary school graduates will do a satisfactory job. If scholarships are intended to provide additional recruits for special areas of our society – scientists, social workers, teachers or missionaries – the tests to be used, and scores which will qualify the accepted candidates, must be tailored to the task.

One could make a brief for examining the subject area competence of students in areas in which they had not had previous schooling. There are undoubtedly students who have learned a great deal about mechanical things through their own curiosity, through recreation and experimentation, through observation and self-directed reading rather than through formal course work. If scholarships encouraged the further development of students such as these, a potential additional source of creative talent might be uncovered. A brief could be made, too, for awarding scholarships to those who are not in the highest ranks of academic promise but who can contribute importantly nonetheless. We award scholarships to students many of whom would go on to college in any event. If instead, potential teachers could be located and subsidized – students who are not in the top ten per cent of their class, whose scores on our usual scholarship tests are mediocre, who would not otherwise pursue further education, who might not earn the highest grades in a teacher training course but who could successfully negotiate a teachers college program and would enjoy teaching – more would be contributed by scholarships for this purpose than by the ego-satisfying but unessential support of those whose careers are not genuinely affected. Lower qualifying scores, or even different examinations, should be employed for this kind of scholarship award.

To summarize: the kinds of tests that are appropriate for college admission and scholarship programs are those which are best suited to the individual institution and the particular purposes of the scholarship donor. No one testing program will suit all schools or all purposes. There are many good tests. It is incumbent on the conscientious user to select from among them those which most nearly meet his special needs and circumstances. Otherwise, the tests which have provided milestones along the road of educational progress may become millstones around the neck of the educational process.

NDEA: Opportunities and Responsibilities in Test Development and Test Use

The potential impact of the National Defense Education Act on the field of evaluation and measurement would be difficult to overestimate. Thousands upon thousands of students have been measured, as a result of this program, in abilities in which they would not otherwise have been measured. Hundreds of school systems have elaborated their testing and guidance procedures in ways which they would not otherwise have seen as possible. Statewide testing programs have arisen where they did not previously exist. The time, effort, and money devoted to testing activities have been enormously expanded, and are likely to be even further expanded in the future. NDEA funds represent a truly major investment in American education. Will this investment fully realize its objectives? Yes, if all those to whom the program offers opportunities accept the accompanying responsibilities. No, if responsibilities go unrecognized. No, if those who direct the utilization of the funds and those who benefit financially from the increased usage of tests and measurements fail to fulfill responsibilities however evident.

Other Beneficiaries

Who is afforded opportunities by the passage of the National Defense Education Act? Primarily, of course, it is the student who is intended as the ultimate, if not direct, beneficiary of the investment; but it is not only the student who will derive direct benefits. There are profits to be made by the publishers of the tests which find favor; there are royalties earned by the authors of the tests. There are budgets in state departments of education, suddenly provided with monies over the expenditure of which

From *Personnel and Guidance Journal*, 1960, 39, 41-44. Copyright 1960 American Personnel and Guidance Association. Reprinted with permission.

the department has considerable discretion, and budgets in local school systems unexpectedly augmented with funds which derive from federal rather than local taxes. For the people who publish the tests, author the tests, or direct testing and counseling activities at the state or local level, the newly available money provides unusual opportunities – opportunities which if seen in narrow perspective can mean immediate financial profit to authors and publishers, and subsidization of pet projects to directors of testing programs, but disappointingly little to the student and the fields of education and measurement; if seen in broader perspective, the financial gains can still be ample, the contributions to budgets can help improve established programs or bring new programs into being, while the primary goals of NDEA and their highly desirable concomitants are being achieved.

Publishers and authors of tests can accept the increments in profits and royalties as simply the proper reward of the ingenuity, skill, artistry, and effort that went into the creation of the instruments, with no feeling of further obligation. It might be suggested that enlightened self-interest would indicate a different viewpoint. The additional profits might well be re-invested in the improvement of the very instruments whose sale yields those profits, in the improvement of other instruments which have not been similarly favored, in the development of new instruments, or in the development of devices and materials which will facilitate the mechanics of the testing process or the interpretation and communication of test results.

Perfection Not Yet upon Us

Even though a test, or a set of tests, has been widely adopted for use in testing programs, it is likely to be susceptible to improvement. There are opportunities for expanding the sizes of normative samples, of obtaining more representative norms, of developing meaningful local norms. There will be new samples on which validity may be studied and new criteria against which to study validity – assuming, of course, that schools will cooperate in such studies. Manuals might well be revised to incorporate the extensive new data and increase the usefulness of the tests.

While we are engaged in revising manuals, publishers and authors ought to consider some of the new conditions under which test results will be used. Particularly, it is important to recognize that the task of administering the tests, and of interpreting the test results, is frequently falling on unprepared shoulders. This is inevitable, perhaps, when the use of tests is so suddenly and so extensively broadened. It is to be hoped, naturally, that in-service training courses and similar methods will be employed to improve the competence of those who have not heretofore been trained in test administration and interpretation. But such training takes time – and, meanwhile, tests are being given and test results are being interpreted. It would seem desirable, therefore, for test manuals to take into account the lack of experience, and of sophistication, of teachers and counselors suddenly faced with new responsibility. Directions for administration will need to be paragons of clarity, with details fully spelled out. The importance of adhering strictly to prescribed time limits must be emphasized. No assumptions can be safely made that teachers will understand the conditions necessary to standardized test administration unless the teachers are explicitly instructed – and even then we can only hope that each teacher has been so motivated as to care whether or not the tests are properly given. This may be an alarmist view, but experience indicates that an alarmist view may be necessary to help forestall the presence on pupil record cards of meaningless scores.

We need to view with at least equal alarm the interpretation which newly drafted counselors and teacher-counselors will make of test scores. For years, measurement authorities and counseling psychologists have lamented the numerous situations in which tests have been given and results then permitted to accumulate dust in untouched files. We may soon be faced with the unpleasant dilemma of choosing between the waste of uninterpreted scores and the dangers of misinterpretation of those scores. The primary responsibility for instructing counselors and teachers in the meaning of test results does not fall on the publisher or author; the manual can, however, play a helpful or harmful role. For example, we know that even some experienced counselors are not thoroughly at home with correlation coefficients; the increased use of expectancy tables can serve to illuminate the meaning of reported coefficients and to stress the probability nature of predictions derived from correlation studies. Since differences between scores are so central to interpretation of test data in counseling and guidance, devices should be employed which will guide interpreters to understanding when found differences have no real significance.

NDEA should provide added stimulation to authors and publishers to develop specialized instruments for specific areas – for example, one such obvious area would be that of aptitude for the learning of foreign languages. Coincident with this opportunity come responsibilities:

1. To provide evidence that the new instruments will predict better than scholastic aptitude tests, or measures of competence in English, or other generally predictive tests;

2. To avoid making claims for new tests until empirical data will support those claims.

As indicated above, the activities of authors and publishers will affect, and be affected by, programs arising from the NDEA. Of far greater influence, however, will be the role played by the measurement specialists in the individual state departments of education and of the consultants whose services they employ. In their hands lies the basic responsibility for the quality of programs in their states. They may choose a highly permissive approach, and let local communities within the state make the significant decisions – but even this choice must represent a judgment that such a plan is the most effective one for that state; otherwise, it is simply a failure properly to discharge the responsibility explicitly assigned by the NDEA.

Optimum Use of Funds

The first deadline for utilization of NDEA funds found many state education departments sorely pressed for time; the many weeks lost while awaiting clarification of the meaning of the Act and of what would constitute approvable programs made hurried action on the part of the states reasonable, if not inevitable. Perhaps the haste served to cause some premature activities, or perhaps it merely served to highlight them. In any event, plans for future programs warrant more mature consideration for the utilization of NDEA funds.

There are instances in which the funds have been used directly or indirectly for the construction of tests by the state education department. If these tests measure knowledge or skills which are not already measured by available standardized tests, this kind of activity may be respected. If, on the other hand, the department's tests merely duplicate what is equally well assessed by well-established scholastic aptitude or achievement tests, the basic purposes of NDEA have been violated. The Act was passed to develop the resources and skills of the nation's students, not to help state officials build empires.

As one looks at the programs adopted by some local communities, and even by some states which have statewide testing programs, one gets the feeling that tests are being selected on the basis of price rather than quality. The assumption appears to be that tests put out by the major publishers are about equally good and all are good enough. The tests are not equally good or equally useful; they differ in orientation, in content, in reliability, in validity, and in appropriateness of norms.

Differences in orientation are perhaps most obvious among achievement tests, where curricular emphases vary widely and where dissimilar subject matter or skills may be encompassed in competing instruments. Important differences also exist among scholastic aptitude tests. One such test may include a numerical reasoning section, another may offer a non-language subtest. A third test may contain verbal, numerical, and abstract subtests, but with all three of these abilities measured by materials differing in kind from the types used in the first two tests. There are one-score cycle-omnibus tests and there are differential aptitude test batteries. And if anyone is unaware that there are very considerable differences between types and within types of scholastic aptitude measures, he need only refer to Buros' *Mental Measurements Yearbooks*, to reviews in the professional journals, or to the manuals accompanying the tests. Tests should be bought on the basis of quality, relevance, and usefulness; the bargain-basement approach has no proper place in professional measurement.

The Need for Standards

The decision as to whether or not there should be a statewide testing program is properly one which each individual state should make for itself. Each state must make the judgment that students will best be served by a coordinated, uniform program across the state, or by leaving to local communities a larger or smaller share of discretion as to how NDEA funds are to be used. If a state chooses to let individual school systems fashion their own programs, the state is still not justified in permitting the adoption of just any kind of program the local community might propose. The state is responsible for the effective use of the funds. Unless it can be sure that every community is genuinely able to exercise good judgment in developing a local program, the state cannot in good conscience surrender complete control to the community. Some devices must be adopted to enable the state to exercise such supervision as is necessary in individual instances.

These devices may range from a non-directive approach reined by veto power over specific provisions, to stating a limited number of satisfactory alternatives from which communities may choose. As applied to test selection, the former approach would be represented by a scheme under which the individual school system would report what tests it proposed to use at each grade level, and the state would veto the use of inappropriate or otherwise unsatisfactory instruments. The latter approach might be one in which the state carefully reviewed the available instruments and specified a restricted list of tests from which communities might select. Whatever the mechanics of control may be, control must be exercised – maturely, professionally, responsibly. The use of any instrument by a community must be such that professional people in the state education department can defend it to their professional peers. The state may delegate to the local school systems the choice of instruments – it cannot delegate the obligation to assure the effective use of the NDEA funds.

Of course, test selection is but one of the activities in which the state has important NDEA responsibilities. The test results will be interpreted; the interpretations will contribute, in many instances, to important decisions by students. Even before NDEA, there were not enough school personnel available with adequate understanding of the meanings of test scores. The rapid expansion in test programs now taking place aggravates the deficiency. In allocating money to individual communities, the state might well consider whether greater good may result from using significant sums for development of competent interpreters, via in-service training courses and the like, than from prodigal underwriting of test administration where test interpretation is likely to be naive or misguided. Wisdom in the utilization of fewer bits of well-understood information may pay greater dividends than unsophisticated treatment of ill-digested masses of test scores.

One final admonition. For many years, whenever the topic of federal aid to education arose, many of us voiced the fear that federal aid would mean federal domination of education. The passage of the National Defense Education Act demonstrates unequivocally that it need not be so. The latitude provided to the states is so great as to render any fear of the bug-a-boo of federal control in this instance groundless. State education authorities have been given the opportunity so to govern the allocation of funds as to make for a maximum contribution to the development of our future citizen, the student. It is up to these authorities and to the psychologists and educators who also benefit from this Act to make the most of the opportunity – to discharge the concomitant responsibilities fully and conscientiously – to justify federal aid without federal control by demonstrating that it is effective, as well as philosophically desirable – in short, to achieve the purposes which brought into being this National Defense Education Act.

Some Effects of Speed in Test Use

If we are to understand the nature of speed as a variable in psychological testing, we must first understand that speed is a dimension rather than a trait. In all too many instances, we find a tendency to reify speed – to think of it as a kind of unitary skill, like strength of grip, which we may expect will function similarly whenever called upon. This way of thinking about speed has led to the inclusion of inappropriate tests in selection batteries and misinterpretation of data in research aimed at investigating the nature of tests. It is our present purpose to illustrate, by examples, how speed is a quite different phenomenon from one setting to another.

Consider the situation in which an industrial organization sets up a test battery for selection of administrative or sales personnel. The first component is usually a test of general mental ability, intelligence, learning capacity (or whatever designation one prefers). Very often this test is one in which speed plays an important role. One reason for choosing a speeded test is, of course, the reluctance of industry to spend any more than minimum time on testing. Another reason frequently offered is that the firm wants men who can think quickly and can make rapid decisions. The implicit assumption is that speed as represented in the test and speed as represented on the job are one and the same. It is a dubious assumption at best. If the test proves valid, it is more likely to be because the test is easy for the bright candidates and difficult for the less able. It is primarily knowing more, not thinking faster, that distinguishes the high scorers from the low. For example, Bennett and Doppelt (1956) matched two groups of applicants to schools of nursing on a vocabulary test. One group was then given a set of easy vocabulary items from an alternate form while the other took a set of difficult items. The experimental tests were administered under speed conditions. The research showed that the less able applicants

---

From *Educational and Psychological Measurement*, 1960, *20*, 267-274. Reprinted by permission.

worked equally slowly on easy and hard items; the more able answered a larger number of the easy items than of the difficult ones. Bennett and Doppelt concluded that there was a definite relationship between the examinee's vocabulary knowledge and her rate of responding to vocabulary test items.

An experiment by McGehee[1] provides similar evidence in a very different setting. A newly-employed group of embroidery punch operators in a textile plant were administered a job-sample test – one which very closely duplicated the job for which they were hired. Shortly after the hiring, production (piece) rates of high and low scorers were obtained; the job-sample test was found to have very considerable validity. However, at the end of a month, production records of high and low scorers were again compared. Group differences in performance on the job had decreased to the point of vanishing, and validity was accordingly approximately zero. Apparently, those who scored high on the job-sample test were the people with prior experience as embroidery punch operators. Those who were not previously experienced did poorly on the test and on the job because they had not yet learned the necessary skills. These skills they learned relatively quickly on the job, and the acquisition resulted in performance equal to that of the previously more experienced employees. Thus, it was the knowledge and skill of both groups of employees which determined the speed at which they performed.

A third example demonstrating the effect of ability or knowledge on speed is chosen from the new Davis Reading Test (F.B. Davis & C.C. Davis, 1957). This test provides two scores: Level of Comprehension, based on the first forty items, which almost everyone answers; and Speed of Comprehension, based on all eighty items, which almost no one completes. In the investigation of test-retest reliability, data were gathered which included Level and Speed scores from alternate forms administered to the same students. From these data, correlation coefficients were obtained to show the relationship of Level of Comprehension scores from form to form, and of Level of Comprehension scores on one form to Speed of Comprehension scores on an alternate form. These coefficients were obtained separately for eleventh and twelfth-grade students, and for college freshmen. In each grade, the average correlation between Level of Comprehension scores from alternate forms was (exactly) the same as the average correlation between Level of Comprehension on one form and Speed of Comprehension on another. Once again, the conclusion seems apparent; speed of performance is determined very largely by the knowledges and skills of students.

The above examples are illustrative of instances in which knowledge or skill is intimately related to speed. Let us now look at some situations in

---

[1]McGehee, William. Personal communication.

which the opposite is the case. The Differential Aptitude Tests (Bennett, Seashore & Wesman, 1952) consist of seven tests which are essentially power tests and one test (Clerical Speed and Accuracy) developed specifically as a measure of speed of perceptual and motor performance. The task of the student who takes the Clerical test makes so little demand on the intellect that very few errors are made by the majority of examinees. The median correlation coefficient between Clerical scores and scores on the other seven Differential Aptitude Tests, for grades eight through twelve, is .13 for boys and .16 for girls. Thus, there is very little relationship between speed of performance on a task which requires little understanding and scores on tests which make intellectual demands on the student.

The chief characteristic of the DAT Clerical Speed and Accuracy Test is that so few errors are made. This characteristic is not, however, limited to clerical tests. Some respected intelligence tests have components which seem almost as simple as the simplest clerical test. Since the original Army Alphas, through the Chicago Non-Verbal and down to the current Wechsler intelligence scales, the digit-symbol test has been an accepted subtest for measuring intellectual power in children and adults alike. Yet the substitution of a digit for a geometric design, with the key constantly before the examinee, is hardly a complex process. The simplicity of the digit-symbol task accounts for the fact that the number of items attempted under the usual speeded administration is almost as good a score as the number of items correctly done. The word "almost" must be used because a very small number of subjects may misunderstand directions or may find even this kind of task challenging their limited mental ability. Thus, Cassel[2] recently made available data on the digit-symbol subtests (I and X) of the Chicago Non-Verbal Examination (Brown, 1936) for 145 boys in a state institutional school. All of these students were classified as having IQ's above 84, and their mental ages ranged from 6.1 to 10.9. On subtest I, only nine of the 145 boys marked as many as seven items incorrectly; all nine of these earned scores of 0-3 where the total distribution encompassed scores up to 59, with a median of 27. The results for subtest X were very similar. Clearly, then, we have here a test which is permitted to contribute importantly to the measurement of intelligence but which is basically a perceptual speed test for a very large proportion of appropriate examinees.

Interestingly enough, although the digit-symbol substitution process does not seem to be much more demanding than is the DAT clerical task, there appears to be a real difference between these tests in their relation to more cognitive tests. In contrast with the average correlation of .13 cited above between DAT Clerical and the other Differential Aptitude Tests, the digit-symbol test (officially called Coding B) in the Wechsler Intelligence Scale for Children (Wechsler, 1949) has for 10-year olds a median intercor-

---

[2]Cassel, Robert H. Personal communication.

relation of .30 with eleven other subtests in WISC; the coefficient of correlation with the Vocabulary test is .41. These coefficients probably support the inclusion of the digit-symbol subtest in an instrument aimed at measuring general mental ability. The difference in behavior between these two simple perceptual tasks makes it difficult to generalize concerning the nature of speed as a variable.

Another way in which speed behaves is as a personality or work-habit variable. In the development of simple perceptual tests like the DAT Clerical, we are likely to assume that students will work as rapidly as perceptual and motor skills permit. This is undoubtedly so for many pupils, perhaps true for most, but certainly not true for all. Early in our experience with the DAT we found that counselors were perplexed by students who scored very well on the verbal, numerical, and abstract reasoning tests, but very poorly on the clerical test. We hypothesized that these were students who were used to checking their test answers carefully to avoid making mistakes, displaying an attitude of stress on correctness often inculcated by teachers. Accordingly forty such youngsters in one school system were retested with an alternate form, and with modified directions which were devised to counteract the hypothesized caution of the pupils. The increases in score were far greater than could be accounted for by regression or practice effect. The group as a whole went from about the fifteenth percentile to well above average; the most dramatic change was that of a boy who scored at the fourth percentile on the first test and at the eightieth on the retest. The test may have been measuring work habits or caution in these pupils, as originally administered; it does not appear to have been measuring the kind of perceptual-motor skill it was intended to tap.

As a related thought, one is reminded that many personality inventories stress that the respondent is to answer each item quickly, or with the first response that occurs to him. It would be interesting to know whether there is accompanying research to demonstrate the validity of this procedure. It seems appropriate to wonder whether, with some such inventories, different responses might be given if directions permitted unhurried, considered answers, and whether those responses might result in different personality trait scores. The writer is unaware of definitive research on this question; he recognizes that as inventories run into hundreds of items there may be discomforting practical consequences in asking the respondent to give full consideration to each and every item. Still, he cannot help wondering.

The field of achievement testing is another in which there have been more assumptions than well-directed research with regard to the behavior of speed as a variable. This topic has been discussed by Cronbach (1949) as follows:

> Another variable which reduces validity of achievement tests is the speed factor. Time limits are often needed for administrative convenience, but

when speed becomes a major element in determining a person's score, the score is likely not to represent his attainment accurately. Speed is a legitimate element in achievement tests only when speed is an objective of the course. Speed is relevant and important in tests of typing attainment or reading facility, or tests of arithmetic for use in hiring cashiers. Speed is irrelevant if we wish to know how large a pupil's vocabulary is, how much science he knows, or how accurately he can reason. In most achievement tests a speed loading can be justified only if the test is to be used empirically to predict success in a task where speed is helpful, or if data are available to prove that scores on the speeded test correlate very highly with scores on the unspeeded test. Speed tests have limited validity for describing the knowledge of individual pupils, since a few well-informed pupils are slow workers.

For our purposes, one might wish that Cronbach had spelled out these principles in greater detail. Thus, one sentence might be expanded to read, "Speed is a legitimate element in achievement tests only when the *same kind of speed which the test is measuring* is an objective of the course." Similarly, he might well have said, "Speed is relevant and important in . . . tests of arithmetic for use in hiring cashiers *if the kind of arithmetic problem is one in which it is necessary for cashiers to be able to operate with speed.*" Unless we have clear experimental evidence to the contrary, we might well assume in any specific situation that speed in the test is justifiable to the extent that the test is a genuine job-sample of the course or job activities for which the test is intended. There are probably satisfactory cashiers in many stores who cannot solve arithmetic reasoning problems with appreciable dispatch.

In any test which is a combination of speed and power, the role which speed plays may be a very confusing one. Let us look at one or two illustrations. As a first example, take the situation in which a vocabulary and reading comprehension test are given with a single time limit. The student who finishes the vocabulary items quickly has more time to spend on the reading passages than the student who works more slowly on vocabulary. The performance of the two students on the reading comprehension section is consequently not truly comparable. As a second example, let us consider a test of "general mental ability" consisting of verbal and numerical items presented in alternating groups. Two students with equal strength in verbal ability and equal weakness in numerical ability may obtain very different scores. The first student may achieve a relatively high score by skipping the numerical items, racing through as many verbal as he can within the time limit; the second student, permitting himself to be slowed down by the more time-consuming numerical items, may earn a much lower score. Seldom will the difference in approach of these examinees bear valid relation to the criterion.

That speededness is incompatible with item analysis has been demonstrated theoretically, logically, and experimentally. As an example of the latter, Wesman (1949) showed that if the seventieth item of a speeded test given to one group of high school graduates had been "write your own name," the item-test coefficient would have been at least .84 and the per cent passing the item no greater than 50 per cent. It is now equally recognized that reliability coefficients based on highly speeded tests are of little or no value, except perhaps to delude the unsophisticated. We know, too, that tests with very short time limits put an extremely heavy premium on exact timing in test administration; a half-minute error will have far greater effect on scores on a two-minute test than on a thirty-minute test. In one midwestern high school, inattention by the administrator to timing on a three-minute test resulted in 99th percentile scores for almost every student in the class.

One of the basic questions to which we do not as yet have satisfactory answers is that of the quotidian variability on different kinds of mental tests from individual to individual. Does the speed with which an individual attacks a test depend on whether the test is easy or difficult for him? On easy tests, such as involve clerical or simple coding tasks, is an individual consistent from day to day, as he usually is on power tests? How much greater is the variability among examinees on such simple tests than is the day-to-day variability within the examinee?

Other basic questions concerning the nature of speed will occur to the psychometrician who seeks to use it as a variable. Questions will be more likely to occur if the assumptions concerning speed are kept to a minimum, and if the experimenter remembers that speed is not itself an ability, but a dimension.

References

Bennett, G.K. and Doppelt, J.E. "Item Difficulty and Speed of Response." EDUCATIONAL AND PSYCHOLOGICAL MEASUREMENT, XVI (1956), 494-496.

Bennett, G.K., Seashore, H.S., and Wesman, A.G. *Manual for the Differential Aptitude Tests.* (Second Edition) New York: The Psychological Corporation, 1952.

Brown, A.W. *Chicago Non-Verbal Examination.* New York: The Psychological Corporation, 1936.

Cronbach, L.J. *Essentials of Psychological Testing.* New York: Harper and Brothers, 1949.

Davis, F.B. and Davis, Charlotte C. *Davis Reading Test.* New York: The Psychological Corporation, 1957.

Wechsler, D. *Wechsler Intelligence Scale for Children.* New York: The Psychological Corporation, 1949.

Wesman, A.G. "Effect of Speed on Item-Test Correlation Coefficients." EDUCATIONAL AND PSYCHOLOGICAL MEASUREMENT, IX (1949), 51-57.

Testing for Differential Aptitudes

A basic definition necessary for this discussion is that of what we mean by aptitude test. The definition I shall use is that an aptitude test is any test which is used for prediction of some type of future learning. This view is not as startling as it might have been a decade or two ago, before "intelligence" tests began to give way in the schools to "scholastic aptitude" tests. Actually, of course, group tests of intelligence used in the schools were devised primarily as measures of scholastic aptitude, and the kinds of items employed (principally verbal and numerical) reflected this intent. Unfortunately, the use of the label "intelligence" – and its ill-begotten offspring, the IQ – deluded too many parents, teachers, and students into treating results from these tests as though overall potential for learning were being appraised. While this naive misconception still persists to some extent, it is far less prevalent than it once was and is happily clearly on the wane. What is measured by "intelligence" tests is now perceived as the measurement of one or two or three abilities which are important in the prediction of success in future learnings – in other words, scholastic aptitude.

Achievement tests, too, should be recognized as aptitude tests. Though generally viewed primarily as recording the past learning by the student, achievement tests are frequently very good predictors of future learning. The same score that indicates how well a student has performed in a subject up to now is likely to foretell quite well how he will progress in the future. Accordingly, achievement tests may act effectively as aptitude tests.

A second basic concept is the notion of "differential" aptitude. This refers simply to the fact that we differ in the abilities we have, and in our prospects of acquiring new knowledges and skills in various fields of endeavor. The counselor who suggests law as a better bet than engineering

From *Educational Horizons*, 1964, *43*, 31-36. Reprinted by permission of Pi Lambda Theta.

for one of his students, and the coach who selects one eighth-grade student to train for high hurdles and another for the hundred-yard dash are acting on belief in differential aptitudes. All of us evidence this belief in various ways in our daily lives. The management of the New York Yankee baseball team demonstrated their belief in differential aptitudes when they took a third-string catcher and made him manager of the team. Ralph Houk validated their judgment by leading the team to three straight pennants.

If we did not differ in our possession of various aptitudes, there would be no need for more than one test of general ability, e.g., the Otis. That test could be given to all students, regardless of their courses or goals; or to all applicants, regardless of the positions for which they were applying. The higher scorer on such a test would be hired for training whether the job was that of bank teller, punchpress operator, artist, or airplane pilot. No sane employer would willingly accept such a classification – or rather nonclassification – approach to selection of trainees; he would look for specific abilities or skills more relevant to, and more predictive for, the particular job involved. This is why tests of clerical aptitude, manual dexterity, space relations, and the like were developed as early as the group tests of mental ability ("intelligence").

As the vehicle for discussing testing for differential aptitudes, I have chosen the test battery which is the most widely used; which has been accorded highly favorable reviews by leading measurement textbooks as well as in that bible of the field, Buros' *Mental Measurements Yearbook;* for which there is more published validity research data than for any competitive series; and of which I am one of the authors – the *Differential Aptitude Tests* (DAT).

The DAT came into being as a result of the conviction on the part of my co-authors (George K. Bennett and Harold G. Seashore) and me that the so-called tests of general intelligence were not general enough; the information they provided was too restricted and the IQ yielded by such measures was all too subject to misinterpretation. We believed that counselors, parents, teachers, and the students themselves needed more information concerning the student's potential than had heretofore been available in "intelligence" tests. Furthermore, supplementing such tests with then available tests of "special aptitudes" (such as mechanical comprehension) would not fulfill the need since the latter were normed on quite different populations of students; thus scores on "intelligence" tests could not be properly compared with those on the "special" aptitude tests to evaluate relative strengths and weaknesses within the individual student. By the same token, scores from different "special" aptitude tests were also not comparable with one another – again, the norms populations were not the same, an essential for comparison purposes.

The DAT, then, were devised to meet these needs. Eight tests were developed to represent eight sets of abilities which, we judged on the basis of previous research and experience, would predict performance in many educational and vocational areas. The eight tests were:

1. Verbal Reasoning:–analogies items in which the initial and final terms of the analogy are both to be supplied by the examinee from sets of options provided in the test.
2. Numerical Ability:–computation and reasoning items intended to measure both skill in manipulation of numbers and understanding of numerical concepts.
3. Abstract Reasoning:–pictorially presented sequences in which the examinee must identify the principle involved in the sequence.
4. Space Relations:–items requiring the examinee to visualize how a pictured pattern would appear if constructed into a three-dimensional object, and to imagine various rotations of that object.
5. Mechanical Reasoning:–pictorially presented representations of mechanical principles and forces.
6. Clerical Speed and Accuracy:–extremely simple letter and number combinations for which speed of perception and response is essential.
7. Spelling:–everyday words which should be part of the vocabulary of an eighth grade student presented in correct form in some instances, and in the most frequent incorrect form in others.
8. Grammar (in earlier editions called Sentences):–items testing the ability to identify incorrect grammar, punctuation, and word usage as these appear in the test sentences.

In addition to scores on each of these tests, a combined V + N score is also derived, for use as an index of scholastic aptitude for situations in which such a measure is needed – ordinarily, as a substitute for a displaced "intelligence" or "mental ability" test.

Obviously not all aptitudes or intellectual skills are encompassed by the DAT; other tests might readily have been incorporated. We felt, however, that practical considerations required some limits as to how much should be included in a single battery; the aptitudes measured were those deemed most broadly applicable to the educational and vocational scene. The entire battery was normed on a single population of students across the country in 1947 and again in 1952, and a revised battery was recently similarly normed on some fifty thousand boys and girls in grades eight through twelve in 43 of 50 states. Thus, the counselor has available a set of aptitude measures, each adequately reliable on the single scores it yields, which are directly comparable for appraisal of within-student ability.

Since their original launching seventeen years ago, the DAT have been the subject of very considerable research. The test scores have been correlated with all kinds of grades in schools across the country; they have been validated against achievement test scores earned in courses taken some time after the aptitude tests were administered; they have been used to predict College Board *Scholastic Aptitude Test* scores two years in advance. Students have been retested after three years to document the stability of the measurements; they have been followed into post-high school educational and vocational careers. Literally thousands of validity coefficients have been reported by the authors alone, while uncounted other validity studies have been reported by independent researchers in educational, psychological, and industrial literature. What have we learned from all this extensive research?

The first observation is that, in general, those tests which an experienced counselor would expect to be predictive in a given subject actually are predictive. For English grades, the Grammar and Verbal Reasoning tests predict best; grades in mathematics and bookkeeping are forecast most effectively by the Numerical Ability test. The Verbal Reasoning, Grammar, and Numerical tests predict grades in social studies courses; the same three tests, together with Abstract Reasoning, are useful for prediction of science grades. Success in learning shorthand is practically always forecast best by scores on the Spelling test; for mechanical drawing and geometry, the Space Relations test scores are very effective.

If one limited himself to the study of only those situations in which test scores were compared with grades in obviously relevant courses, however, much valuable information would be lost. For a second observation is that tests often predict effectively in courses for which they may appear to have little relevance. For example, the Numerical Ability test turns out to be effective for predicting grades in such unexpected courses as English, social studies, mechanical drawing, typing, and foreign language. Presumably, the general reasoning component of the Numerical Ability test accounts for this relationship since there is little or nothing in course content to lead us to anticipate this correlation.

In view of our cultural stereotype, the next generalization may be somewhat surprising:—girls are more predictable than boys, at least as far as school grades are concerned. This generalization does not apply, of course, for all classes or subjects; no generalization does. By and large, though, as we inspect summary tables of validity data for the DAT, the greater predictability of girls' grades comes through with remarkable consistency. Moreover, this observation holds not only for courses we usually associate with girls' interests and abilities, such as English and social studies; it holds equally for what are considered "boys' courses," such as mathematics and science. Why this should be so may provoke interesting conjecture; one reasonable guess, for example, may be that girls may conform better to teachers' demands, completing homework assignments promptly, requiring less disciplining for classroom misbehavior, and the like. Unfortunately, our research does not explain the phenomenon; it merely documents, quite unmistakably, that the phenomenon exists.

One of the most important demonstrations which the thousands of validity coefficients provide is that of the specificity of validity. Despite the emphasis of every good measurement text on the fact that the validity of a test is specific to the school, the subject, the criterion, and the students on whom the validity coefficient is based, test manuals continue to report single coefficients of validity for a course or occupation as though that lone coefficient represented the prediction which other users of the test might expect. That such an implication is completely unwarranted is well illustrated by even the most cursory inspection of summary tables in the DAT Manual. For example, the first sets of validity tables in the third edition of the Manual report coefficients of correlation between each of the DAT scores and grades in English courses – in 43 different courses for boys, 41 different courses for girls. For the Verbal Reasoning test, the highest reported coefficient for boys is .78; the lowest is .11. Suppose that only one of these coefficients had been reported – the prospective user of the test would be severely misled as to the kind of prediction he might expect in his own situation. As it happens, the median of the 43 coefficients for boys is .49, and for the 41 studies of the girls is .52. These are far more indicative of what the user may expect than a selected high coefficient would be.

Why is validity so specific? The tests, obviously, are constant – they remain the same regardless of the students to whom they are administered. Equally obviously, however, the courses are *not* the same; though all may be called "English" courses, some may focus on grammar and the mechanics of language, others on literary appreciation, and still others on creative composition. Courses called "mathematics" may include general mathematics, with emphasis on numerical computation and problems involving calculation of interest, or advanced algebra, trigonometry, statistics, and similar subjects demanding appreciation of abstract mathematical symbolism. Biology, chemistry, and physics, each with its unique subject matter and intellectual demands, are but three of the courses subsumed under "science." It would be utterly unrealistic to expect any test, or any series of tests, to show constant relationships with such varieties of criteria.

Sectioning procedures are also responsible for some of the specificity of validity. In some schools, where sectioning is practiced, students are placed in rapid (or "enriched") programs, regular classes, or slow-learner groups, and are exposed to different course content. It is hardly surprising that tests should be related differently to grades earned under these varying conditions.

The sectioning process tends in itself to affect validity coefficients by depressing them. It is a psychometric fact that the narrower the spread of ability within a group, the smaller will be a correlation coefficient between a measure of that ability (whether teachers' grade or achievement test score) and a relevant predictor. Since the essential goal of most sectioning is to produce relatively homogeneous groups, it is to be expected that validity coefficients will be smaller than they are when sectioning is not employed.

One should not leave the topic of why grades are differently predicted, from class to class and school to school, without noting one of the most prevalent reasons. This is the age-old disposition to reward students for promptness, neatness, cooperation, and similar virtues which, though highly laudable, are only indirectly related to genuine attainment of academic knowledge and skills, and are not predictable – nor is there any intent to predict them – from aptitude test results.

Despite these and other difficulties, prediction is effectively accomplished, as is demonstrated by the large number of sizable validity coefficients reported in the DAT Manual, and by the results obtained by independent researches. A recent study undertaken by the University of Minnesota Student Counseling Bureau for one of the schools in the statewide program brought to our attention an excellent illustration of differential aptitude prediction. At the beginning of the ninth grade, 383 students in this school took the DAT; they then went on into algebra and geometry courses. Of particular interest are validity coefficients for three of the DAT against grades earned in these two mathematics courses. The Numerical test predicted algebra and geometry grades equally well, the respective coefficients being .58 and .59. Differential prediction should lead us to expect, however, that neither the Space Relations test nor the Mechanical Reasoning test would predict equally well for these courses; in keeping with their intended purposes they should be more effective predictors of performance in geometry. The expectation was realized in this study. The validity of the Space Relations test was .27 against algebra grades, but .42 against geometry. Similarly, the respective coefficients for the Mechanical Reasoning test were .07 and .31. Clearly, the unique components in geometry were associated with relevant components of these two tests.

Since the overall theme of this program session is "Innovations in Testing," it is perhaps incumbent that I remark on at least one or two more recent developments. One successful recent venture is the *Modern Language Aptitude Test*, prepared by Professor John B. Carroll of Harvard University and published by The Psychological Corporation. Until recently, despite a number of efforts at development of prognostic tests of ability to learn a foreign language, the most successful predictive instruments were "general intelligence" tests or English language usage tests. Professor Carroll set himself the task of producing an aptitude test which would be directed at specific language learning skills, and thus to measure different relevant characteristics than were encompassed by IQ or grammar measures. That he was successful is demonstrated by the comparison of validity coefficients obtained by use of Carroll's MLAT and of the Otis test on the one hand, and the DAT Grammar test on the other. In one school, Otis Beta IQ's predicted language course grades to the extent of a .52 validity coefficient; for MLAT the coefficient was .71. In a second school, against a similar criterion, the DAT Grammar test showed validity of .35; for MLAT the coefficient was .55. Clearly MLAT is measuring aptitudes which are in part, at least, different from those in this test of mental ability and this test of language usage.

A field in which there is much ongoing activity is the attempt to measure creativity. Since in virtually all such efforts the researchers seek to demonstrate that what is being measured is a quality not appraised by intelligence or scholastic aptitude tests, this is another contemporary instance of testing for differential aptitudes. I would like to report some clear success in these endeavors, but the research which has come to my attention thus far permits no such happy conclusion. Where the evidence is satisfactory that the quality measured differs from what other aptitude tests measure, there is doubt that what is being measured is creativity. It may well be that the central problem has been ignored heretofore, namely – what is creativity? Several of my colleagues at The Psychological Corporation believe that a satisfactory definition, acceptable to authorities in various fields of endeavor, is necessary before fruitful work on the measurement of creativity is possible.

To study the criterion, they have devised a number of paragraph statements of hypothetical, imaginary events, each of which describes an activity which may be deemed creative. The situations described are then to be classified along several dimensions: area (arts, business, or science); significance or triviality; time (short or protracted); responsibility (individual or group); and training (whether the achievement was that of a trained or untrained person or group). After the items have been matched in an appropriate experimental design, the entire set will be submitted to eminent persons in business, science, and government for ratings of each imagined situation as evidencing creativity. From studies such as this, it is hoped that a satisfactory definition of creativity may be evolved; this criterion may then serve to focus development of more satisfactory tests of creativity than are presently available.

In summary, testing for differential aptitudes is a natural, almost inevitable, outgrowth of our experience with "intelligence" or "mental ability" tests and progress in our understanding of the structure of intellect. We the people differ widely in our possession of various abilities, and in our potential for acquiring new knowledge, skills, and understandings, both educational and vocational. As long as these differences exist, it is important to measure them and to utilize the information gained from our measurements for the fullest benefit of each individual's development.

Review of the Iowa Tests
of Educational Development

The *Iowa Tests of Educational Development* were prepared to "provide a comprehensive and dependable description of the general educational development of the high school student.... With respect to all broad aspects of educational development that are readily measurable, the *Iowa Tests of Educational Development* meet this need .... [The tests] emphasize ultimate and lasting outcomes of the whole program of education.... [They are] not... limited to the temporary and immediate outcomes of instruction in individual subjects." Thus, the announced goals more directly resemble those of the *Sequential Tests of Educational Progress* (STEP) than those of more directly curriculum-oriented batteries like the *Stanford Achievement Test* or the *Metropolitan Achievement Tests*.

To achieve these goals, nine tests are employed drawing on the subject matter of four broad curricular areas: social studies, natural sciences, general mathematics, and English. Social studies is represented by two tests: a 90-item conventional test called Understanding of Basic Social Concepts and an 80-item reading test called Ability to Interpret Reading Materials in the Social Studies. Two parallel tests represent natural sciences, each with the same respective number of items. The single mathematics test consists of 53 problems and is called Ability to Do Quantitative Thinking. English is broadly represented by tests of Correctness and Appropriateness of Expression (99 items), Ability to Interpret Literary Materials (80 items), General Vocabulary (75 items), and Use of Sources of Information (60 items). There is also a composite score including eight of the tests (all but Use of Sources of Information). The 707 items and 26 reading passages require almost eight hours of working time, or two full school days (9:00 A.M. to 3:35 P.M.) of testing. A "class period" version takes five and one half working hours over two less crowded days.

From Buros, Oscar Krisen, Editor, *The Sixth Mental Measurements Yearbook*. Highland Park, N.J.: Gryphon Press, 1965. Pp. 51-55.

The required investment of pupil and school time would seem to make it mandatory for administrators to consider whether or not there is adequate return for the expenditure involved. Among the specific questions to be answered are: How much information are we getting? How useful is the information for direct improvement of the pupil's education? Might equally good information about the student's ability be obtained in less time, or more varied useful information in the same amount of time? If the information is obtained for the pupil in one year, is there enough change in the abilities appraised to justify testing with the same instruments the following year and the year after that – for four years if the manual's recommendations are followed; or would new and different information about the pupil be a more profitable investment? When schools are being accused from within and from without of overtesting, such questions may not be lightly dismissed.

On the whole the tests are prepared with satisfactory technical competence. There has been a genuine effort to include items which call for the ability to generalize, to apply in new situations what has previously been learned in other settings, and to derive information from newly presented materials. The success of this effort varies from test to test; Understanding of Basic Social Concepts and General Background in the Natural Sciences are liberally sprinkled with "fact" items, as is Use of Sources of Information. The vocabulary test and the spelling portion of the correctness and appropriateness test are conventional measures of these fields of knowledge. Accordingly, it is primarily in the three reading tests, and perhaps in the mathematics test, that the student's ability to generalize and apply principles is challenged.

The scoring and reporting services which are an integral part of the SRA-scored program (half the Manual for the School Administrator is devoted to preparations to be made for testing, checking in materials, shipping test materials, using a grid on the answer sheet, and the like) are attractive; they should save schools the otherwise heavy burden of scoring the tests and preparing rosters. Moreover, a school system which wishes to have basic statistics computed for various groups to be studied may order these statistics as part of the reporting service. Hopefully, the availability of these computational services will increase the likelihood that administrators will devote serious attention to the results of the testing program.

The widespread use of this battery indicates that a great many school administrators have been impressed with the ITED program. Test specialists are unlikely to find comparable satisfactions. One source of dissatisfaction is the lack of restraint exercised in putting forth claims; that the claims are sometimes inconsistent with one another appears not to have acted as a deterrent. Thus, the tests are proposed to school administrators "to provide a dependable and objective base for evaluating the curriculum programs of individual high schools" and to "point up any need for curriculum revision that may exist"; for teachers and counselors the tests "will be useful in educational guidance and in the adaptation of instruction to individual needs." These virtues are professed despite the information that the tests were "not constructed on the basis of an analysis of the content of any specific high school courses."

Further, the tests "are designed for administration to all students in the school, regardless of their grade classification or course registration," even though they "measure education development in [only] four major curricular areas." Again, though the tests are presumably independent of the curriculum, "there is some advantage in giving the tests early in the school year, in order that ... the measures may be influenced as little as possible by the temporary results of current instruction." The reader who brings into apposition these conflicting statements from the various pamphlets and manuals must be pardoned his confusion.

The claims go on and on. The battery, we are told, "identifies students for possible grouping and/or special project assignments"; it "makes it easier to adapt instruction and guidance to each student's unique and changing needs." It measures "the knowledge and skills the student has accumulated from all [sic] of his in-school and out-of-school experiences." It will help the student "make up your mind how to distribute your efforts in your schoolwork." These are but a few of the benefits purported, in the various manuals, brochures, pamphlets, and bulletins, to flow from the use of tests. The claims are overwhelming; unhappily, they are largely unsubstantiated.

What about the tests as tests? The "heart of the battery consists," we are told, "particularly of tests 5 through 7. Tests 5, 6, and 7 measure the ability to interpret reading materials in the social studies, the natural sciences, and literature." In effect, then, we have here three reading tests drawing on content from three curricular areas. The list of skills the tests are intended to measure is very similar to the lists of skills to which the standard single reading tests are also addressed. The closest approach to uniqueness is found in those passages and items of the natural science reading test which deal with reports of experiments. No equally distinguishing characteristics appear in the other two reading tests. One need not gainsay the indisputable importance of reading as a central skill to question whether 240 items and three hours are appropriate expenditures; one hour or less is ordinarily sufficient to obtain satisfactory measures of a high school student's speed and level of comprehension.

The specific content of certain of the individual tests is to be reviewed by other contributors to this yearbook. This reviewer is impelled to express the wish that more careful editorial attention had been devoted to some of the items. For example, in Form Y-4 of the quantitative thinking test an item reads, "The first four values in a series of numbers written according to a set scheme are" and this is followed by *five* numbers. In the same booklet, the social studies reading test contains purported excerpts from five writers, numbered I, II, II [sic], IV, and V. Since the correct answer to the second item on this passage is "Writer III" and one of the misleads is Writer II, the student may well be perplexed. It is also somewhat disconcerting to find, in the basic social concepts test, an item stem which concludes with "What explanation may be offered for this?" Literally, of course, *any* explanation may be *offered.* This may appear to be "nit picking," but anti-test critics make much of such lapses. One has come to expect more attentive care than is displayed in these and similar instances.

Perhaps the most serious deficiency of the ITED program is the failure to provide the kind of statistical data to which the interested potential user is entitled. There is no single manual to which one may refer for basic information; one must flit back and forth among the Manual for the School Administrator, the Manual for Teachers and Counselors, a bulletin on using the ITED for college planning, and the scoring keys (the only source for raw score to scale score conversion). The end product of this flitting is, unhappily, frustration.

The Manual for the School Administrator contains two reliability tables, the correlation coefficients being of the odd-even variety. One of these tables refers to Form X and Form Y; no further identification is provided. It appears most unlikely that the exact same coefficients would have been obtained for Forms X-1, X-2, and X-3, or for Y-1, Y-2, and Y-3. The reader should not be asked to assume that these coefficients apply to the particular form with which he is concerned. No information is presented, either, as to the means and standard deviations associated with these coefficients. Presumably the coefficients refer to the full-length versions of the battery; in that case, no data are presented for the shorter class-period versions. A school which used these tests could not readily judge whether or not these coefficients were based on a more heterogeneous group than its own, and might therefore be larger than would be the case for that school.

Absence of basic information also characterizes the other reliability table; again, no means or standard deviations are provided. This table does identify the forms studied as X-4 and Y-4 and presents odd-even reliability coefficients for the full-length and class-period versions. A comparison of these coefficients will leave the reader more than a little puzzled; the full-length versions appear to be no more reliable than their class-period portions! No coefficient for the full-length version is as much as .05 larger than that of the class-period segment; in fact, in several instances the coefficients for the shorter versions are larger than those for the full-length. Undoubtedly, there is a reasonable explanation for these unreasonable data; one may assume, perhaps, that the standard deviations of scores for the groups which took the shorter versions were larger than those for the groups which took the full-length version. If so, the importance of reporting standard deviations is cogently illustrated. As reported, the coefficients range between .81 and .96 for the individual tests for a single grade; the composite score reliability is estimated as .98.

Much is made, in the Manual for the School Administrator, of the care taken to assure representativeness of the norms sample for the 1957 standardization. It is entirely likely that the group used for the development of norms compares favorably with samples used for competing test batteries. The presentation of the data, however, is most unfortunate. Tables derived from U.S. Office of Education census data are presented as percentages. Tables showing similar breakdowns by region, community size, and grade for the ITED norms are shown as frequencies. When these frequencies are translated into percentages, discrepancies between census data and the norms tables are revealed to be of considerable size. For example, the census proportion of high school students in the East South Central region, in small communities, is reported as 65 per cent; only 26 per cent were obtained for the ITED standardization. Similar discrepancies appear for other portions of the sample. It is not the reviewer's contention that these discrepancies mean that the normative sample is poor. Had the manual simply described the sample obtained in objective fashion, there would probably be little cause to comment. It is because the manual places the stress it does, with implicit claims, that the discrepancies become noteworthy.

What of validity, that most central quality of a test? Validity of the ITED, we are told, cannot be described on any quantitative, objective basis. The tests are declared, however, to have predictive guidance value; the demonstration of predictive usefulness does call for evaluation, by validity coefficients or similar evidence against the criteria which the tests purportedly predict. In the Manual for the School Administrator, no coefficients appear; nor are any to be found in the Manual for Teachers and Counselors. In the latter, there is the statement that the composite score serves quite well as a predictor of academic success as measured by school marks, and reference is made to "studies summarized in Part III of the Manual for the School Administrator." But studies are *not* summarized in the manual referred to – at least, not in the 1962 edition made available to the reviewer. Instead, one is again referred – this time to a special bulletin, Using the Iowa Tests of Educational Development for College Planning.

The latter bulletin reports validity coefficients for the composite score against freshman performance in a number of colleges; most of the coefficients reported are very respectable. (The presence of standard deviation data for some of the studies is most welcome.) The validity coefficients suggest, as one should expect from a battery of such length, that the composite score is a good predictor of college grades. The relationship of ITED twelfth grade composite and quantitative thinking scores to College Board scores is also reported, and is appreciable ($r = .80$ to $.87$). No data from earlier grade (more useful) administrations of the ITED are cited. The bulletin notes that ITED provides limited discrimination above SAT scores of 550. This is perhaps not unexpected, since ITED is presumably aimed at average students, not only the college-bound. At the same time, the usefulness of the ITED for counseling with respect to the more selective colleges is accordingly limited.

One section of the bulletin which should be of appreciable interest to counselors of college-bound students presents the ITED profiles of high school students who subsequently were graduated from college in various major fields; within each field, separate profiles are shown for students who earned "A," "B," and "C" averages. Though limited to Iowa colleges, and though some of the n's are inevitably small, the follow-up study as a whole is very much a noteworthy contribution. One cannot help but wish that here, since means and standard deviations for the separate tests are reported and criterion grades were obviously at hand, validity coefficients had also been computed; they have not.

This kind of failure to present relevant data, even when these have clearly been available, typifies the program. It is well-nigh impossible to understand why more information concerning the tests and their use does not appear in a comprehensive manual. Millions of students have taken these tests in recent years; opportunities for extensive research are practically built into the reporting services offered to the schools. Why, one wonders, have these opportunities been so neglected? Why are there not long tables of validity coefficients for each of the tests against appropriate criteria? Why are there not test-retest data from successive administrations – the schools are urged to test the same students four times during their high school years. Where are the tables of intercorrelation with other tests? Where is the evidence that sufficient growth occurs in the abilities measured by these tests to justify urging schools to duplicate testing year after year?

The *Iowa Tests of Educational Development* are among the most widely sold tests. According to the publisher's announcements, over a million and a half high school students take this battery each year. The very size of the program emphasizes the obligation of the authors and the publisher to provide superior tests, complete documentation of psychometric characteristics, substantiation of claims, and a body of research data consistent with such widespread usage. Too much of this obligation is unfulfilled.

Because the *Iowa Tests of Educational Development* include three reading tests, and because there is absence of evidence that full-length versions have more to offer than class-period versions, this reviewer feels the battery is inefficient. Nevertheless, a school system may deem what is measured by the tests (as distinguished from what is claimed for them) is worth obtaining as testimony of certain kinds of achievement; in that case, administration of the battery once during a student's career would be warranted. Until evidence is presented that noteworthy gains occur from one year to the next, the reviewer believes that expenditure for retesting is wasteful; the time and money might better be devoted to testing for other abilities, aptitude or achievement, which will yield new and useful information.

ADDENDUM. In late February 1964, several months after the above review had been submitted to the editor, the publishers made available a revised Manual for the School Administrator, dated December 1963. The revised manual contains a more satisfactory discussion of the topic of validity (except for cavalier treatment of "concurrent" validity), but the evidence offered to document validity of the ITED is still most disappointingly meager, especially in view of the extraordinary wealth of opportunity to do and report studies of this characteristic. Means and standard deviations are still conspicuous by their absence from all tables in the manual; thus, the interpretation of tables of reliability, intercorrelation, and correlation with scholastic aptitude tests remains ambiguous. Tables reporting reliability data are similar to those presented earlier, and subject to much the same criticism. The discussion of the standardization population differs from the earlier discussion; it is more elaborate, but no more satisfactory. In the circumstances, the reviewer is not impelled to modify appreciably the general conclusions represented in the original review.

Intelligent Testing

The nature of intelligence has been a favorite subject for contemplation and disputation for centuries – perhaps from the dawn of man as Homo sapiens. The topic is being studied and debated today by educators, sociologists, geneticists, neurophysiologists, and biochemists, and by psychologists specializing in various branches of the discipline. Despite this attention and effort, however – or perhaps *because* of it – there appears to be no more general agreement as to the nature of intelligence or the most valid means of measuring intelligence than was the case 50 years ago. Concepts of intelligence and the definitions constructed to enunciate these concepts abound by the dozens, if not indeed by the hundreds.

With so many diverse definitions of intelligence, it is perhaps not surprising that we cannot agree on how to measure intelligence. It is my conviction that much of the confusion which plagued us in the past, and continues to plague us today, is attributable to our ignoring two propositions which should be obvious:

1. Intelligence is an attribute, not an entity.
2. Intelligence is the summation of the learning experiences of the individual.

We have all too often behaved as though intelligence is a physical substance, like a house or an egg crate composed of rooms or cells; we might better remember that it is no more to be reified than attributes like beauty, or speed, or honesty. There are objects which are classifiable as beautiful; there are performances which may be characterized as speedy; there are behaviors which display honesty. Each of these is measurable, with greater or lesser objectivity. Because they can be measured, however, does not mean they are substances. We may agree with E. L. Thorndike that if something exists it can be measured; we need not accept the converse notion that if we can measure something it has existence as a substance.

Intelligence as here defined is a summation of learning experiences. The instances in which intelligent behavior is observed may be classified in various ways that appear to be logical or homogeneous, but they are individual instances all the same. Each instance represents a response the organism has learned; each learned response in turn predisposes the organism for learning additional responses which permit the organism to display new acts of intelligent behavior.

For our present purposes, it matters little whether we are more comfortable with stimulus-response bonds, with experience-producing drives, with imprinting, or with neuropsychological explanations of *how* or *why* learning occurs; whatever the learning theory, the fundamental principle is universal. We start with an organism which is subject to modification by interaction with the environment; as a product of that interaction, the organism has been modified. Further interaction involves a changed organism – one which is ready to interact with its environment in a new way.

Organisms may differ from one another in their susceptibility to modification. One organism may need a more potent stimulus to trigger reaction to the environment than does another. A particular organism may respond to a given class of stimuli more readily than it does to other kinds of stimuli. Organisms may differ from one another in their readiness to respond to different classes of stimuli. There may be important differences in the ability of organisms to modify their behavior in effective ways as a result of experience.

We may develop and investigate hypotheses as to whether such differences in response as are displayed arise from variations in neurological endowment or in conducive environment. All that we can be sure of, at least as of now, is that what we are dealing with is a response-capable organism which has been exposed to environmental stimuli, has interacted in some way with those stimuli, and has been modified thereby.

The bits or modules which constitute intelligence may be information or may be skill; i.e., they may be content or process. Furthermore, they are multidimensional, and some modules may have more dimensions than do others. Each module is subject to essential change as the individual is exposed to further learning experiences. Each act of learning serves to create new modules, change the existing ones, or both. Modules are not independent; rather, they may overlap with several or many other modules; thus, they are complex both in their number of dimensions and in their interrelationships. Even early percepts are rarely if ever simple. A toy ball when first seen has at least size, shape, and color; if it is touched, it has texture and hardness as well. Accordingly, few if any modules of learning are truly simple.

The whole of a person's intelligence at any given moment may well be thought of as an amorphous mass – not a regular geometric figure. Within this mass, modules may cluster with greater or lesser permanence, and may be organized along principles of relatedness. Thus, word knowledge may form a cluster – but the words of which one has knowledge will be components of other clusters as well. A pencil is an object one writes with; it has shape in common with other objects, it has function in common with pens and crayons, it produces color of varying intensity, it has a number property, it is usually associated with paper. The learned module "pencil" may thus be part of many clusters.

One need not posit that a learning module is permanent. It could, presumably, disappear entirely, although far more often we would expect it to undergo essential change by taking on a more complex character. This model does assume that higher learning depends so intimately and essentially on certain previous learnings that the more complex modules cannot exist without the antecedent modules from which they grew. For example, if the ability to subtract numbers should disappear, the ability to do long division could not remain unaffected. Thus, retention of learning is integral to the concept here proposed.

The simple-minded conceptualization outlined above may have horrified those of my colleagues who are even moderately sophisticated with respect to modern learning theories. To those colleagues I apologize, but I also beg their indulgence. Oversimplified as the conceptualization undoubtedly is, I believe it does no *essential* violence to any current theory; it has, I hope, the virtue of permitting a view of the organization of intelligence, and of the nature of the testing of intelligence, which may prove illuminating for several issues which confront us.

Issue I: The Classification of Ability Tests into Aptitude, Achievement, and Intelligence Measures

As soon as we have agreed that what we know and what we can do intellectually is learned, the artificiality of the above classification becomes self-evident. Historically, we have recognized that what achievement tests measure is what the examinee has learned. We have been less ready to accord similar recognition to intelligence tests. In their case, we have too often behaved as though what these tests measure is somehow independent of the learning phenomenon. We have played the role of Aladdin seeking a magical lamp, complete with a genie ready to spring forth with full power to accomplish all sorts of wondrous things. We have pondered wistfully on the number of critical issues that would be resolved if we could only somehow measure "intelligence" separately from "achievement."

We have been similarly unrealistic in treating the concept of "aptitude." Our textbooks enunciate the distinction that aptitude tests measure what the individual *can* learn, while achievement tests measure what he *has* learned. Some of our leading theorists aggravate the confusion by ignoring the implications of their special use of the term. "Aptitude" is typically used in laboratory learning experiments as a matching or otherwise controlling variable; it is employed to assure that groups to be compared start the experiment as equal in initial ability. One gets a strong impression that the aptitude instrument is perceived as measuring the innate potential of the individual as distinguished from what is to be achieved (i.e., learned) in the experimental process. If learning theorists recognize that what they are calling "aptitude" (or, for that matter, "intelligence") is "previously learned" (as, clearly, at least some of them do), the artificiality of the distinction between "aptitude" or "intelligence" and "achievement" should be eminently apparent.

I wish that at least a few of my psychometric colleagues would leave off searching for *the* structure of intelligence, and devote their wisdom and energy to learning more about the learning process, and to teaching learning theorists about testing. I am convinced that both specialties would profit immeasurably from the cooperative enterprise. It is my strong impression that the inattention of the psychometrician to the facts of learning is matched fully by the unsophisticated treatment accorded to testing by many learning theorists.

All ability tests – intelligence, aptitude, and achievement – measure what the individual *has* learned – and they often measure with similar content and similar process. Let us take, for example, an item[1] such as this: A square and a rectangle have the same perimeter. The square has an area of 10,000 square feet. The rectangle has an area of 9,324 square feet. What are the dimensions of the rectangle?

This item would clearly be deemed appropriate whether it appeared in an achievement test in high school mathematics, a test of aptitude for mathematics, or the numerical portion of an "intelligence" test. I submit that a great many items can equally readily fit any of the three categories.

Such justification as we have for our labeling system resides entirely in the *purpose* for which the test is used, not in the test document itself. If our intent is to discover how much the examinee has learned in a particular area, such as a school course, we may select items which probe for the distinctive learnings the schooling was intended to stimulate. We label the

---

[1]This item was proposed by G. K. Bennett in another context as an example of an arithmetic problem which might be correctly answered by any of several methods.

test an "achievement" test. If our intent is to predict what success an individual is likely to attain in learning a new language, or a new job, we seek those specific previous learnings the possession of which bodes favorably for that future learning, and we label the test an "aptitude" test or a "special aptitude test." If our intent is to predict future acquisition of learning over broad areas of environmental exposure, we seek those previous learnings the possession of which will be relevant to as many, and as important, future learning situations as we can anticipate. This test we label an "intelligence" test. The selection of test items or sample tasks for the three purposes may or may not differ; but in each instance what is measured is what was previously learned. We are not measuring different abilities; we are merely attending to different criteria. It is the *relevance* of the learnings we select for investigation that largely determines how we name our test, and whether we will succeed in our purpose.

Issue II: The Utility of Culture-Free and Culture-Fair Tests

The notion of relevance of previous learnings leads naturally to a consideration of some follies we have committed in the search for culture-free or culture-fair instruments. I do not wish to impugn the high social motives which stimulate the search for such devices; I do wish to question that such a search, in its usual setting, is sensible. A culture-free test would presumably probe learnings which had not been affected by environment; this is sheer nonsense. A culture-fair test attempts to select those learnings which are common to many cultures. In the search for experiences which are common to several different cultures or subcultures, the vital matter of relevance of the learning for our purpose is subordinated or ignored.

The implicit intent in the attempt to create culture-free or culture-fair tests is somehow to measure intelligence without permitting the effects of differential exposure to learning to influence scores. This contains the tacit assumption that "native intelligence" lies buried in pure form deep in the individual, and needs only to be uncovered by ingenious mining methods. If we recognize that intelligence comprises learning experiences, it becomes clear that our attempts are not ingenious, but ingenuous.

It is true that we can probe learnings that have occurred in nonverbal, nonnumerical domains. This means only that we can test selected aspects of intelligence. The question immediately arises of the relevance of these special domains to the kinds of learnings we will want to predict. The measurement purpose for which culture-fair tests are ordinarily developed is that of predicting academic or industrial performance. Most academic courses and most industrial jobs involve some use of verbal abilities. Since further learning is conditioned by relevant past learning, the individual who has developed more of the prerequisite ability inevitably has an advantage over the individual with less of the prerequisite ability. If we wish to predict whether an individual will profit appreciably from additional exposure to learning, our best predictor must be a measure which appraises what prerequisite learning he has acquired heretofore. Appropriate verbal abilities are more relevant to the largely verbal learning we usually wish to predict than other abilities are.

It has on occasion been suggested that tests be developed which sample the verbal skills or factual information which are peculiar to a given subculture. Such tests are proposed as a "fairer" measure of the "intelligence," or readiness to learn, of the members of that subculture. The response to this proposal is "readiness to learn *what?*" If our purpose is to distinguish members of that subculture from their peers with respect to how much of that special culture they have assimilated, such a test might well be useful. If, as is more likely the case, we wish to predict future learnings of the content of the more general culture (e.g., the so-called white, middle-class culture such as typifies what the majority of our schools are organized to transmit), tests designed for the subculture will be less relevant than those which sample from the general culture. This is not intended to imply that the members of the subculture *could* not learn what the schools as constituted are offering. It does emphasize that, at the moment at which we make our appraisal, what the individual has already learned from the general culture domain is the most significant information as to what he is then ready to learn. The less relevant the previous learnings we appraise, the more hazardous must be our predictions of future learnings.

As long as our educational system and our general culture are dependent on conventional verbal abilities, those who aspire to progress in that system and that culture will need to command those abilities. In a verbal society, verbal competence cannot sensibly be ignored.

Issue III: Is "Verbal Ability" Synonymous with "Intelligence"?

To say that we cannot afford to ignore learnings in relevant verbal areas when we are appraising "intelligence" does not imply that *only* the verbal domain is important. The development of tests of "general mental ability" which sample only the verbal domain implies that since verbal tests predict school criteria best, it is unnecessary to attend to other cognitive abilities the student has developed; in other words, that, in effect, "verbal ability" is synonymous with "intelligence." It would be most unfortunate if, consciously or unconsciously, we adopted this too narrow perspective.

That verbal tests are typically good predictors of grades in many academic courses is undeniable. *Why* this is the case warrants some thought. Is it because all, or even most, of what constitutes "intelligence" is represented by verbal ability? Certainly the chief symbol system of our society is verbal. Even when we deal with numerical, spatial, or figural problems we often transform them to verbal expressions. It is one thing, however, to recognize the involvement of verbal abilities in all kinds of learning experiences and quite another to grant them exclusive sovereignty over learning domains. Many domains require the possession of other abilities as well, but our appraisal methods are often inadequate to reveal that need. Because it is easier to employ verbal criteria, or more convenient – or because we have given insufficient thought to criterion validity – we predetermine the finding that verbal abilities dominate the scene.

A particularly revealing demonstration of this phenomenon came to the attention of the authors of the Differential Aptitude Tests some years ago. Grades in an auto mechanics course were found to be better predicted by the Verbal Reasoning test of the DAT than by the Mechanical Reasoning test. We had the unusual good fortune of having access to further information about the course. We discovered that early in the course the teacher had been called from the room for almost a half-hour. In his absence, the students had disobeyed his instructions not to fool around with the automobile motors. To let the punishment fit the crime, he conducted the rest of the course almost entirely by lecturing, giving the students minimum opportunity for actually working with the engines. That grades in a course taught by lecture and evaluated by a written test should be best predicted by a verbal test is not too surprising!

An illustration such as the above should force us to stop and think. As we study tables replete with validity coefficients, how many of those coefficients represent similar instances? As we develop hypotheses as to the importance of particular aspects of intelligence, how well do we understand the *criteria* which gave rise to the coefficients on which our hypotheses are based? Would the use of more valid criteria in courses for which curricular goals transcend verbal skills, have produced similar data, or different? Would the admittedly broad pervasiveness of verbal skills seem quite so broad if more appropriate measures of learning were employed? If we remain complacent about criteria composed largely of behaviors from the verbal domain, we are unlikely to see the relevance of other abilities.

In his APA presidential address in 1964, McNemar paid flattering attention to the Differential Aptitude Tests; he quite accurately reported that the verbal tests were most frequently the best predictors of course grades. The data he cited certainly supported the point he was making: Verbal tests predict grades in many academic courses. What might well have been added was recognition that the nature of our educational criteria exaggerates the real importance of verbal skills. If (and it is hoped *when*) grades or other criterion statements become more content valid, the relevance of a number of other skills will be more demonstrable.

Industry has perforce learned this lesson. Few mechanical apprentices are selected solely, or even primarily, because they can describe a process, rather than perform it. The military has learned that the ability to diagnose a malfunctioning torpedo is poorly demonstrated by verbal exposition, but well demonstrated by a work sample requiring actual mechanical repairs. It is to be hoped that education will increasingly become more realistic with respect to what *its* criteria *should* be.

Issue IV: The Growth and Decline of "Intelligence"

So preoccupied have we been with reifying intelligence as some mystical substance that we have too often neglected to take a common-sense look at what intelligence tests measure. We find ourselves distressed at our failure to predict with satisfactory accuracy the intelligence test scores of a teen-ager from his intelligence test scores as an infant. Why should this occasion surprise, let alone distress? If we look inside the tests, it should be obvious that the kinds of learnings we typically appraise at the earlier ages bear little resemblance, and may have little relevance, to the kinds of learnings we appraise later.

At the earlier age levels, we have typically tested for such characteristics as motor dexterity, perception, and similar features of physical develop-ment. When intellectual concepts become available for testing as baby grows to infant, to child, to teen-ager, we change the focus of our testing from the physical domains to the cognitive – we appraise knowledge, concept formation, and reasoning.

It is possible that future research will disclose that possession of certain physical abilities or tendencies is prerequisite to the development of concept formation, and that earlier possession of these characteristics will foretell the future intellectual development of the individual. Interesting and promising research now being conducted is directed toward this goal. It is my opinion that, because learning experiences vary so from one child to another, there is some practical limit beyond which we will be unable to predict, however penetrating our research. In any event, we would do well at this moment to recognize that since we are measuring in different ability domains at infant and school-age levels, we should not expect good prediction from one level to the other – and we should certainly not behave as though the data permitted confident prediction.

At the other end of the age spectrum we have, with similar lack of insight, proceeded to corollary errors. We have accepted the gloomy dictum that once we have passed the age of 18, or 25, or 35, we have passed our peak; from that age, our ability to learn declines. Our texts are peppered with charts showing that depressing downhill slide. What is the basis for this widely accepted conclusion? The principal basis is that when we apply our conventional measures of intelligence to older people, we find that average scores decrease. We have implicitly accepted the idea that intelligence is defined by what is measured by these particular intelligence tests. If, however, we return to our previous formulation of intelligence as what we know in a wide variety of domains, and hence as a base for what we can learn at a given moment, our perspective changes. We then proceed to compare what the intelligence tests measure with the kinds of learning individuals have engaged in from age 30 or 40 on. The relevance of the tests, except perhaps as measures of retention, is seen as increasingly remote with each passing year. Most individuals have not failed to learn more with added years of life. Their learnings have occurred in areas (science, business, politics, psychology, psychometrics), often relatively specialized, which are not measured by conventional intelligence tests.

It is true that new learnings of adults occur in such a variety of endeavors that it would be virtually impossible to find a common core on which all could be examined. We should not, however, pretend we do not suffer this psychometric disability; we should not continue to use less relevant measures to support deceptive graphs and curves of the decline of "intelligence." We might better recognize the limitations of our measure, until such time as we can devise relevant measures of the significant learnings which do occur. For the present, we can conclude only that with each passing decade older people do less well on tests designed for younger adults.

Issue V: The Search for Purity

A discussion of the nature of intelligence, and of intelligent testing, should not ignore the topic of factor analysis. It is a method which has influenced test construction and test selection. It is a technique which has stimulated the promulgation of theories of the structure of intellect.

The history of psychometrics gives evidence that each new major technique has attained a heyday of popularity, during which unrealistic hopes led to unbridled use. In the 1920s and 1930s, Pearson product-moment coefficients held the stage; everybody seemed to be correlating everything with everything else with wild abandon. We appear, in more recent times, to have been engaging in factor analyses with almost equal frenzy. With so much activity going on, it is perhaps to be expected that some studies, and some conclusions, would be characterized more by enthusiasm than by wisdom.

To criticize factor analysis as a procedure because individuals have misled themselves through its use would be very silly indeed. Among the benefits it has provided are the ability to summarize vast masses of data, and to facilitate the organization of information in a way that inspires, and then leads to investigation of interesting and often fruitful research hypotheses. At the same time, we need not believe that the power of the tool assures the validity of the product. Some of the conclusions which have been drawn, some attitudes which have been adopted, and some theories which have occasionally been treated as though they were established fact might well be exposed to scrutiny.

There have been instances in which a test battery was chosen for practical use *because* it had its origins in a program of factorial research. Presumably, the rationale was that such a battery consists of relatively "pure" tests, and would show near-zero intercorrelation among the tests; it would therefore be more efficient than a battery of similar measures not derived from factorial studies. If this rationale survived empirical study, it would still not of itself be adequate justification for selecting one set of tests rather than another. Efficiency is certainly desirable – but *validity* is *crucial*. How tests were constructed is interesting and even germane; how they *work* is the critical issue.

Let us return, however, to the rationale. Is the leap from "factorial origin" to "purity" defensible? The "pure" tests developed in psychometric laboratories often do correlate very little with one another. To some degree, at least, this low correlation is frequently ascribable to the unreliability of short, experimental tests, or to restriction in range of the various abilities of the subject, or both. For exploratory and research purposes, these conditions represent a reasonable situation. Practical test use situations are something else again.

When batteries of reliable tests with factorial ancestry, and batteries testing in similar domains but not factor oriented, are given to the same students, the within-battery intercorrelation of scores is ordinarily of about the same order. For example, with one ninth-grade group of boys, the average inter-*r* among the Differential Aptitude Tests was .37; for the same group, the average inter-*r* of the Primary Mental Abilities Tests was .36. Similar results were obtained in a comparison of the DAT and the General Aptitude Test Battery scores for a twelfth-grade group. Thus, there was little evidence of greater "purity" in the factorially derived batteries than in the DAT, which were not so derived. (In the everyday world, it appears, "purity" is all too likely to be an illusion.) Accordingly, we would be well advised when choosing tests for practical use to concentrate on how they work, not on how they were built.

Let us now turn briefly to the role of factor analysis as a stimulator of hypotheses concerning the structure of intellect. Its influence has often seemed to be not so much mathematicodeductive as mathematico*seductive!* The power of the method as a way of manipulating great masses of data appears all too often to have led us astray. Even our more eminent protagonists of the technique have not always appeared immune. When expounding on the theory of factor analysis, experts almost invariably agree that factors are merely descriptive categories; they are not functional entities. But when engaged in interpreting the factors which have emerged from their studies, some analysts apparently succumb to the mystic charm of rotating axes and perceive entities which, they have told us, do not exist. The lure of the temptation to discover a psychological structure analogous to the periodic table of the elements is too powerful to resist. We then hear of "primary mental abilities" or are shown "the three faces of intellect." Though the authors of such creations have sometimes demonstrated in other writings that they well understand the difference between the reality of descriptive categories and the illusion of underlying entities, some of their disciples and many of their readers seem less clear in their perception.

If we accept the thesis that the modules or bits which constitute intelligence are themselves complex, a combination of such modules can hardly be expected to be simple or "pure." A 6-year-old who assembles three alphabet blocks to spell out "cat" has employed, at a minimum, verbal and spatial skills; if he is aware that there are three blocks or letters, he has engaged in numerical perception as well. The ability to perform the task has required cognition, memory, convergent thinking, and evaluation. The product is figural, symbolic, and semantic. All this, and we have not yet taken into account such considerations as the motor-manipulative activity, the perception of color, the earlier learning experiences which enabled him to perform the task successfully, or the imagery which the concept "cat" induces in him. We, as analysts, may choose to attend to only a single aspect of the behavior – but the behavior itself remains multifaceted and complex. To assume that we can abstract from a host of such activities a pure and simple entity is to ignore the psychological meaning of intelligent behavior.

Let us continue to explore, by all means available to us (including factor analysis) the nature of man's abilities. Let us *not* assume that the results of research obtained under closely managed conditions in the laboratory will hold true as realities in day-to-day situations. Let us not unwittingly forget that the descriptive categories we adopt for convenience in communication do not have real existence as ultimate psychological entities.

Conclusion

To what view of a structure of intellect am I led by the ideas I have enunciated here? Essentially, I believe intelligence is *un*structured. I believe that it is differently comprised in every individual – the sum total of all the learning experiences he has uniquely had up to any moment in time. Such structure as we perceive is structure which we have imposed. We can so select samples of previous learnings to examine as to reveal a general factor, or group factors, or specifics. We can sample from domains that are relatively homogeneous and apply labels such as verbal, numerical, spatial; we can sample from a wider variety of learnings, and apply labels such as "general mental ability" or, simply, "intelligence."

There are many bases on which we may choose which kinds of learnings we will sample. The most reasonable basis, I believe, is that of predictive purpose. Those previous learnings should be probed which are most relevant to the particular future learnings we wish to predict. In addition to criterion – or, more likely, *criteria* – relevance, the principles of band width and fidelity (as enunciated by Cronbach and Gleser) might well serve as guides. If we are interested in forecasting narrow-band criteria, selection of highly homogeneous, directly relevant behaviors is indicated. If we are interested in a wide range of criteria, we have at least two options: we may choose to select small samples from widely scattered domains – as in a Binet, a Wechsler, or a broader gauge instrument still to be devised – or examine more intensively with several narrower gauge tests, as in the Differential Aptitude Tests. The broader gauge instruments will offer economy, but lesser fidelity for selected criteria. The narrower gauge instruments will be longer and more time consuming – but the possibility of more direct relevance to one or more particular criteria should permit higher fidelity.

The critical issue, then, is not which approach measures intelligence – each of them does, in its own fashion. No approach save sampling from every domain in which learnings have occurred – an impossible task – fully measures intelligence. The question is rather which approach provides the most useful information for the various purposes we wish the test to serve. Recognition that what we are measuring is what the individual has learned, and composing our tests to appraise *relevant* previous learnings, will yield the most useful information. We, and those who utilize the results of our work – educators, personnel men, social planners – face problems for which intelligence test data are relevant, and sometimes crucial. We must remember, and we must teach, what our test scores really reflect. The measurement of intelligence is not, and has not been, a matter of concern only to psychology. It has always been, and continues to be, an influence on educational and social programs. If we are to avert uninformed pressures from government agencies, from school administrators, from the courts, and indeed from psychologist colleagues, we must understand and we must broadly communicate what these scores truly represent. Only then can we who build tests and they who use them properly claim that we are indeed engaged in intelligent testing.

The Role of the Publisher with Respect to Testing for Employment Purposes

The role of the publisher of industrial tests derives in large part from who or what the test publisher is. If, as is the case for The Psychological Corporation, the publisher is a professional organization, the role is defined in terms of the profession. Essentially, the publisher should be someone who entered the measurement field because of interest in what tests are, what they can do, how to improve them and how to influence their use. He should be committed to the idea that tests are the most desirable means of obtaining certain kinds of information about individuals; that they are more reliable, more valid, more free of bias, more socially desirable than alternate means of appraisal; that they are, in fact, one of psychology's most significant contributions to society and a proper source of pride for the profession of psychology. This is not to say that the publisher-psychologist is unaware of the limitations of the instruments he offers; he is not. But he is also aware of the weaknesses in alternative methods of obtaining the kinds of information tests are specially designed to elicit, and knows that tests hold up very well indeed in any comparisons.

The superiority of tests as devices for gathering information about the individual's abilities has been acknowledged for years. Why do we repeat now what has for so long been recognized? Because tests are under severe attack from government, from the press, from civil libertarians and from within the psychological profession itself. The burden of that attack is that tests are unfair to minorities, unduly depriving the members of minority groups of access to jobs they could successfully perform. The proposed remedies vary from urging that better validation data – especially differential validation data – be obtained, to pleas for different kinds of tests, to demands that testing be outlawed entirely. Beset by colleagues and courts

From *Conference on the Use of Psychological Tests in Employment (Particularly with Minority Group Members)*, University of Rochester, Rochester, N.Y., 1972.

alike, the publisher can well paraphrase Gilbert and Sullivan's policeman – truly, his lot is not a happy one.

How does one review the present state of affairs? Perhaps he starts first with attending to concerns about the "disadvantaged" – this is the aggrieved group, presumably, at the center of the maelstrom. As he directs his attention to the problem, he is immediately faced with a long series of questions. Who are the disadvantaged? Are they those who are black? Are they women, white or black? Are they everyone who is not white? Do they include whites at poverty levels? Do they include professional and middle-class blacks? Do they include blacks with high upward social mobility drives, who instill in their children the will to learn and to succeed?

Is disadvantage purely a matter of socio-economic status? If so, how did so many foreigners who came to these shores impoverished and often ignorant of our language – and sometimes but modestly competent with their own – find a solid place among the "privileged" of their own or succeeding generations? Is it purely a matter of color? Is the son of a black retail store clerk more or less disadvantaged as compared with that of a third generation West Virginia welfare recipient?

The point of the above is not to gainsay the stark fact that there are thousands, or hundreds of thousands, or millions of disadvantaged in our country; one would have to be extraordinarily stupid and hopelessly blind not to be aware of their presence. Rather, these questions are posed to remind us that the term "disadvantaged" is too loosely used; it is too ambiguous. In any setting where rigorous thinking or sound research is to be undertaken with the disadvantaged, the need for clarification of the meaning of the term is urgent.

Unclear as the term "disadvantaged" is, even less clear is it who speaks for the disadvantaged. Who has the right to be their voice? Is it the militant black psychologist who urges the use of standardized tests so that educational intervention may be applied in the effort to overcome educational deficit? Or is it the *more* militant black psychologist who demands that testing be abandoned in its entirety because tests are a millstone on black aspirations? Is it the leader who advocates a fair share for blacks in our present society or the one who has given up on our society and seeks radical change or destruction? Is it the leader who wants the blacks to have proper opportunity to be a part of the majority culture, or the leader who wants a separate culture? To whom is the publisher to listen? Whose demands should he try to meet – as publisher, as professional and as responsible citizen?

Of course, it is conceivable that the publisher will not be permitted to decide whom he will heed, or what his goals are to be. Legislators can prescribe and proscribe and determine the destinies of the publishing activity. They can outlaw all IQ tests or all ability tests. The judiciary can saddle the use of tests with such onerous requirements as to effectively eliminate them from the industrial scene. Governmental agencies can so thoroughly harass test users as to seriously discourage, if not eliminate, the use of selection tests.

On what basis will these agencies arrive at their decisions? Will there be statesmanlike decisions reached as a result of judicious review of the total picture, or will there be yielding to strident political pressures? Will we be so caught up in the social consequences of testing as to be distracted from the social consequences of *not* testing? The answers to these and similar questions may well have a final say in what the publisher can do – and in what his role as publisher is to be.

Viewing the scene as it appears at the moment, it would be all too easy to yield to pessimism. Testing, as we have seen, is assailed from all sides. The Equal Employment Opportunity Commission is expanding its activities at a headlong pace – this summer plans were initiated to hire 200 additional attorneys to prosecute suits, many of which will involve employment testing. Obviously, these attorneys are not expected to sit idly by; work will be found for them to do. Industry must anticipate a broadscale campaign aimed at its personnel practices and must be prepared to pay all the accompanying costs in time and money for preparing a defense for its procedures. To add to its burden, it will most often be dealing with field representatives who are relatively innocent of psychometric understandings; they will have been chosen for devotion to a cause, not for professional competence. It is noteworthy that the announcement reporting the plan to hire the 200 attorneys was not accompanied by indications that similar numbers – or proportional numbers – of psychologists were to be added to the staff. One cannot escape the impression that the intent is not to understand, but to sue.

The influence of the Equal Employment Opportunity Commission has recently been bolstered by victories in the courts. The EEOC's success in its earliest suits occasioned no surprise; its targets were selected with care that they be maximally vulnerable. More recent successes in the courts have been won when the targets appeared less vulnerable. Perhaps the most notable of these was the Griggs vs. Duke Power Company case. In this case, a high school diploma or passing scores on the *Wonderlic* and on the *Bennett Mechanical Comprehension Test* were required for assignment to various entry jobs or transfer from Labor or Coal Handling to more desirable jobs. A district court had found these requirements acceptable. The Supreme Court, however, overturned the junior court's decision.

Some of the principles enunciated by Chief Justice Burger in delivering the decision of the Supreme Court are of prime significance. For example, the statement is made that the Civil Rights Act of 1964 "proscribes not only overt discrimination but also practices that are fair in form, but discriminatory in operation. The touchstone is business necessity. If an employment practice which operates to exclude Negroes cannot be shown to be related to job performance, the practice is prohibited." Further, "Congress has placed on the employer the burden of showing that any given requirement must have a manifest relationship to the employment in question." Further, again, "The administrative interpretation of the Act by the enforcing agency (that is, EEOC) is entitled to great deference."

Though anti-test groups greeted the decision jubilantly, there was basis for satisfaction on the part of test people in the decision as well. Thus, the Court points out that "Nothing in the Act precludes the use of testing or measuring procedures; obviously they are useful." Also, "Congress has not commanded that the less qualified be preferred over the better qualified simply because of minority origins. Far from disparaging job qualifications as such, Congress has made such qualifications the controlling factor, so that race, religion, nationality and sex become irrelevant." These statements offer reassurance to most psychologists and personnel people and, of course, to industry generally.

There was something in the decision for lawyers, too – at least for those who depend on ambiguity to provide the bases for future litigation. The Court neglected to define the term "business necessity"; it deliberately avoided ruling on the question of whether tests may be required that take into account capability for the next succeeding position or related future promotion; it omitted any indication of how related a job-related test must be. (It also referred to "basic intelligence," a concept with which psychologists have had many problems, but which the Court apparently felt no difficulty in understanding.)

It is to be expected that as the Commission finds increasing support from the Congress and the courts, it will expand its attacks to larger industrial organizations with better records of employment practice than characterized earlier targets, and to smaller businesses than have heretofore been investigated. The outcomes of litigation in the next few years will in all probability be the most important single influence on how tests are used in industry.

Additional travail for testing, and thus for test publishing, comes from attacks by psychologists. These attacks may take the form of published research, or they may be editorial argumentation. It is important that I clarify the labeling of research as attack. Proper research, properly executed and properly interpreted, cannot and should not be construed as attack, however unfavorable the results may be with respect to test use. If appropriate tests fail to demonstrate utility in a given situation, that is a fact, not an attack. If tests are chosen inappropriately for use in a given situation, and their failure to demonstrate validity is generalized to situations for which the tests may be appropriate, that is an attack – and an unfair one. If improper statistical methods are applied to analysis of data, that may be an unfortunate lapse, rather than an attack. However, when such analyses are perpetrated by a psychologist who has identified himself philosophically and consistently as opposed to employment testing, one must question the intent as well as the methodology.

The other kind of attack on testing from within the profession takes the form of editorial criticism. Some psychologists are so intent upon eliminating testing from the industrial scene that they ignore the evidence with respect to the demonstrated utility of tests. This kind of criticism is politically damaging but can be met professionally by referring to the data. Other psychologists acknowledge that tests have indeed been useful in personnel selection and that they are as indicative of the abilities of blacks as of whites. They argue, however, that despite these facts there are overriding considerations – that the social need to put blacks on payrolls so they can break out of the confines of poverty is so great that industrial efficiency must and should be sacrificed as necessary to that goal. This is not an argument for psychometricians to meet; it is a matter of urgent, fundamental social philosophy. Whatever the decision may be, however, the elimination of testing is undesirable and, long term, unlikely. If tests are abandoned as devices for selection, they will still have important roles to play in identifying areas in which unselected employed need remedial training and in placing employees in jobs for which they have most promise.

One of the most vexing problems that besets the publisher is presenting satisfactory evidence of the utility of tests. Considering the obstacles to be overcome and the difficulties in performing adequate studies, it is not surprising that tests often fail to demonstrate validity in various industrial applications – the surprise is that they *are* found useful as often as they are.

First and foremost, we need to acknowledge that in many instances the tests simply do not have any useful predictive power – even when the tests have been chosen on apparently reasonable bases. There are situations where what the tests truly measure and what the job really requires are simply not the same – and the coefficients reflect that unhappy fact. All we can do is to look for different tests or accept the notion that these particular criteria are not susceptible to prediction by tests.

The more frustrating situations are those in which there is good reason to believe that the tests are indeed describing relevant characteristics of the examinees correctly – yet there is that in the situation which prevents the worth of the test from showing itself. One such situation is that in which there has been considerable restriction of range – particularly if the test has itself been the instrument employed to bring about that restriction. If that is the case, we may have a test which is working well, yet is described as having little or no validity. The only way the publisher can demonstrate that the test is really working is to persuade the employer to continue administering the test but to disregard the results in hiring decisions. The employer's response to such a request is most likely to be, "You gotta be kiddin'." The EEOC may be able to persuade an employer to disregard scores on a test he believes or knows to be useful; the publisher can't.

One step which is available to the publisher is to persuade the employer to keep a record of scores earned by all applicants – non-hires and non-shows as well as those who land on the payroll. Given favorable circumstances, an estimate of the validity coefficient which would have been obtained had the test not been used for selection can be derived. Sometimes this is a satisfactory corrective. More often, the conditions are such as to minimize or exaggerate or otherwise render meaningless the corrected coefficient; then, it is merely one more instance of frustration. There is the situation too in which scores are important up to a cutoff point, but of little importance beyond that point. Without picking up the low score end of the distribution the presence of validity cannot be documented.

In many, perhaps even in a majority of, circumstances in which tests are used validity coefficients are clouded by the quality of the criterion. Since the nature of the criterion is to be the subject of Dr. Dunnette's talk, I shall not undertake an extended discussion here. At the same time, I cannot forgo pointing out that without a satisfactory criterion there can be no effective prediction – and that studies in which satisfactory criteria are available are very few and far between. Much more often, the criterion is composed of unreliable or invalid ratings, or is addressed at aspects of the job for which tests are not relevant; or, the study is based on so small a number of cases as to require improbably high coefficients to achieve statistical significance. No matter how accurately tests may be describing the abilities they are designed to appraise, and even though the jobs call for those abilities, the results of studies incorporating weak criteria will report failure for the tests. The now classic report by Ghiselli that tests are of but modest predictive power might well be re-interpreted as demonstrating criterion weaknesses instead. When we recognize the factors which militate against demonstrations of validity, it is remarkable that the publisher has any positive evidence to offer at all.

This matter of statistical significance deserves some additional comment. We have developed conventions around stringent significance levels; if a difference between measures, or of a measure from zero, is not large enough to be significant at the 5 per cent level at least, it is dismissed as unimportant. Worse still, it may be interpreted as meaning that the two measures are equal. There is good reason for establishing a sought-for level of significance in the conduct of scientific research. There is also good reason for applying understanding rather than blind adherence in the interpretation of statistical results. Data should provide us with bases for appropriate action, not determine that action for us. What is the inherent magic in a 5 per cent level of significance? Suppose that the likelihood that a given result occurred by chance is only one in eighteen, or even one in fifteen, rather than one in twenty – should the difference between one in eighteen and one in twenty be regarded as significant? Given the necessity for making a decision, is it reasonable to dismiss data that offer odds of fourteen to one or seventeen to one in a given direction but accept odds of nineteen to one? I submit that a validity coefficient which is significant only at the 8 per cent level of confidence deserves almost as much credence as one at the 5 per cent level. For many purposes I would advocate providing a statement of significance level attained to accompany each coefficient instead of classifying all coefficients as worth one asterisk, two or none.

The availability of validity coefficients for reports to users is, of course, vital to test publishing. As we have said, they are hard to come by. The current pressures to report not only validity data, but differential validity data, have increased the publisher's problems enormously. The difficulties in accomplishing studies of differential prediction are many. There is, for example, the problem of numbers of cases to be dealt with. There are few jobs in few companies which have sufficient numbers of individuals employed and subject to the same work conditions and appraised by the same superiors to be worthy of practical study. When we add the proviso of further fractioning according to ethnic classifications, the situations susceptible to study become very few indeed. But suppose we find ourselves with enough cases to permit study, then what? Then, very likely, we will be plagued with criterion questions of a personal kind – the fairness of ratings across ethnic groups. There are those who hold that only blacks can fairly appraise blacks. If that is the case, how comparable are ratings assigned to black and white workers – and what does this bode for attempts to do differential prediction? If what is encompassed in the criterion data is not the same for whites and blacks, attempts at differential prediction change in meaning. We are not predicting differentially for differing ethnic groups, but for differing criteria. Perhaps we must restrict our attempts at differential prediction in its usual sense to situations in which objective production measures are the criteria – and hope that the production measures have real meaning. Practices in which employees are encouraged to keep down their production rates – or even contribute some of their product to less capable co-workers – can impose severe limits on the assessment of validity.

In a recent talk, Mary Tenopyr made some comments worth repeating. "A hypothesis of differential validity could mean that different ethnic groups use different abilities to do the same job. It also could mean that tests measure different abilities for different ethnic groups – or it could mean both. I can find no suitable scientific theory to support such bases for a hypothesis." Continuing, she says, "Bob Guion has suggested that he believes differential validity to be a myth in most cases, but that we should still continue to look for it. I disagree somewhat. I think that differential validity has been something of a pipe dream."

I do go along with Bob Guion on this latter viewpoint, rather than with Mary Tenopyr. I agree that the overwhelming thrust of the data speaks for absence, not presence, of differential validity. Yet I am not ready to abandon research in this area. It is conceivable, at least, that different people may use different abilities to accomplish the same goals. Cultural imprinting could conceivably provide different sets of dissimilar but equally relevant abilities. I do not expect that this will be the case; I am merely willing to grant the possibility. Though the large bulk of good studies speaks firmly and clearly for absence of differential ability, the number of studies is not nearly sufficient to reject the hypothesis that in some situations such differences may appear. It is too early, I feel, for us to be confident we have approximated the universal negative. There *could* be something to this notion and we should not declare research on the topic out of bounds. At the same time, we would do well to recognize that the burden of proof should now rest on those who espouse differential validity as a doctrine, not on those who believe blacks and whites behave similarly on appropriate employment tests and employment criteria.

Now what are the responsibilities of the test publisher with respect to employment testing, and particularly with regard to minority groups? His first responsibility is to publish tests to measure abilities which are important for satisfactory job performance. The special condition imposed by sensitivity to the use of tests with minority groups is that the tests be not only maximally job-related, but that they be minimally culture-laden with non-job-related materials. Items which reflect the learnings of the majority in our culture but are non-predictive of job success are unfair to minority groups; they also evidence poor test construction. This is not to say that items on which whites do better than blacks, or men do better than women, are necessarily inappropriate. If they bear positive relationship to legitimate job criteria, such items may properly be included. If, on the other hand, they attest only to the possession of uncorrelated information, more relevant and more fair items should be substituted for them. A mechanic might better be tested on his understanding of the principles of levers than on whether he knows what RSVP means. A white "chitlins" test is no better than a black one. However, not every item, or every test, must be face valid for each job. Items, or tests, may be predictive of success even though their relevance may not be apparent. The key features are whether there is a genuine relationship with success and whether the criterion is legitimate. Obviously, a criterion which is irrelevantly culture-dominated is not a legitimate one. At the same time there are situations for which familiarity with various aspects of the culture is necessary to satisfactory job performance.

A further responsibility of the test publisher is to report research documenting the situations in which his tests have proved useful, and those reasonable applications in which the tests have not proved useful. I hasten to include the term "reasonable" in my previous statement because of the many woeful instances every publisher encounters in which his test is administered to groups for which it was not intended, or compared with criteria for which it is irrelevant, and is accordingly found wanting. If the *Bennett Mechanical Comprehension Test* fails to predict success of auto mechanics, the publisher feels obliged to report that fact. But suppose an industrial consultant, who should know better but doesn't, gives the lowest form of the test to a group of mechanical engineers. They display very little variability in test scores, with most of them answering virtually every item correctly. The not surprising absence of validity demonstration should not be considered worthy, let alone necessary, to report. Similarly, if a personnel man chooses to give the DAT Space Relations Test to file clerks, and fails to find validity, this need not be recorded in a test manual.

You will have recognized the strong temptation for me to say that if the criterion is composed of supervisors' ratings, since they are often an invalid and unreliable criterion, the results need not be reported. But that temptation must be resisted. Unfortunately, the supervisors' ratings are generally the criterion on which industry relies for its judgments of an employee's success; whether or not he keeps his job may depend on just such ratings. Like it or no, ratings must be accepted as reasonable and the publisher may report the results with explanations – but report the results he must. Nobody ever promised him a rose garden, or manna from heaven, or reliable and valid criteria. Besides, if he is really lucky, they may turn out to be predictable – or even contaminated!

The next area of responsibility of the publisher of tests for industry is the dissemination of norms data for as many different groups as he can manage. Whereas with educational testing national norms are generally the most useful, for employment purposes those that are most likely to be helpful are the most specific. The relevant comparisons are with test scores of those currently on the job as secretaries, welders, salesmen, supervisors, junior executives, and so forth. When there is occasion to report educational norms for industrial tests, these too should be as specific as possible – to region, to kind of school or kind of curriculum (e.g., general academic, technical, trade or commercial), to sex, to grade. The more specific the group on which norms are based, the better able will the employer be to select the norms which most closely resemble the population with which he is dealing.

Perhaps the most important function of the publisher with respect to norms is to encourage the test user to develop his own. These are the most relevant data the employer can have. They are the ultimate in useful specificity. Of course, many employers will have difficulty in preparing dependable norms because they employ relatively few people for any single job. Sometimes it will be feasible to develop norms by combining groups performing similar work, when there are too few in the identical operations. As a general principle, local norms are best and employers should be strongly urged to develop them.

The principle inherent in the above leads to a conclusion with which I am personally unhappy – that separate norms also be prepared for blacks. I do not like the assumption that blacks are different from whites in those characteristics our tests are designed to measure. However, I am forced to face up to certain unpleasant truths in our society – that blacks as a whole have been provided with poorer educational opportunities; and that the impoverished environment in which many grow up will have affected their performance on our tests. Thus, just as I propose separate norms for academic and for vocational students, I feel constrained to follow the logic to separate black norms. (I should say here that not all of my colleagues agree with this position.) Of course, if it should be found that differential validity exists for whites and blacks in a given situation, that fact alone would require the establishment of separate norms, or at least separate expectancy tables. Even if no differential validity is found, however, separate distributions for blacks seem justified for those situations in which the employer may wish to increase the proportion of blacks on his rolls; he should be able to select the higher scoring blacks if he can.

Another area of responsibility for the industrial test publisher is that of helping the consumer understand the meaning of test scores. If he plays this role conscientiously, he is likely to find himself providing interpretive help on testing in general, not just on the tests he himself offers. The publisher should not be expected to provide a measurement course in each manual. At the same time, he should recognize that many personnel people have had inadequate, if any, training. Accordingly, he must explain the meaning of measures at least to the point where routine interpretations of scores will be essentially correct. The manual cannot be merely a set of directions for administration and scoring; nor is it enough to present mere tabulations of reliability, validity and normative data. The manual should guide the user to appreciation of the meaning of the statistical data. As one illustration, the use of expectancy tables as well as validity coefficients is an effective way to improve score interpretation.

Most publishers do not limit their efforts to help the consumer to the issuance of test manuals. Advisory services are available at The Psychological Corporation – I won't speak for other publishers on this point – to respond to specific questions our test users may raise. These sometimes develop into minilectures when the customer's need becomes evident and the service has the time to provide them. Where more elaborate help is needed, the Corporation can sometimes provide professional consulting, whether to help install a testing program or to design validity studies; when the demand exceeds our facility, we ordinarily can recommend competent professionals to serve this function.

Further help to the test user is provided by the publication of bulletins or leaflets which undertake to illuminate measurement concepts in less technical form than that in which they typically appear in textbooks. As an indication of their popularity and presumed success, I can report that literally millions of our Test Service Bulletins have gone to students of tests and measurements or in counseling courses through their professors; with reprints, several individual issues have each exceeded the million copies distributed mark. There seems little question that the profession has accepted them as effective devices for improving test score interpretation.

With specific reference to testing of minority applicants, the publisher should strive to insure, to the extent he can, that the testing situation permits the candidate to demonstrate his actual ability. Two activities of The Psychological Corporation will illustrate this principle. The first of these is called the *Test Orientation Procedure*. This was devised in response to the concern expressed by colleagues that many blacks have been infrequently exposed to the test-taking situation and that the lack of familiarity handicaps their test performance. The *Test Orientation Procedure* consists of a variety of test items which the potential examinee can practice on, and even take home for discussion with family, friends or more experienced test takers. We have no data to prove that the device actually improves performance. We do have the firm conviction that any effect it has is in the direction of improving the validity of scores on tests taken "for real."

The second activity is called CAST. This is an acronym for *Controlled Administration of Standardized Tests*. It was developed in response to concerns that the clarity of the voice conveying directions for taking tests might affect the examinee's performance, and that in situations where prejudice was going to be exercised it might take the form of providing too little or too much time on tests where speed is a factor. CAST is a system composed of tape players. It permits automatic administration of tests, with clearly enunciated instructions being uniformly recited to every examinee. Timing, being controlled by tape, is accurate to a fraction of one per cent. The tape is equally insensitive to shapely legs and black skin; all examinees are given the tests under exactly the same conditions. Practically any industrial test can be accommodated by the CAST system; not only have The Psychological Corporation's industrial tests been adapted to CAST presentation, but so have those of other publishers as well as proprietary tests of various industrial organizations. CAST can not regulate test content; it can and does insure fair administration of tests given by means of it.

Now that we have examined the attacks and some of the treatments applied to our ailing tests, what is the prognosis? Short-term, it leaves something to be desired. There is little question but that civil rights activities have diminished, and are continuing to diminish, the use of tests. It is fashionable for opponents of industrial testing to claim that the use of tests in industry is increasing. The corollary claim is that industry rushed to install testing programs to circumvent the Civil Rights Act. What is the evidence? According to a study published by the Bureau of National Affairs under the auspices of the American Society for Personnel Administration, the opposite is the case. Whereas in 1963, nine out of ten companies surveyed reported using personnel tests, only 55 per cent reported using them in 1971. This is a very significant drop. Nor is there reason to believe the trend will reverse in the immediate future. Companies faced with pressure from EEOC and the courts will decide in increasing numbers to abandon testing rather than face harassment and shoulder the considerable legal costs involved in even a successful defense to a suit. Too many will decide it just is not worth the time and effort. This will include not only firms which would have difficulty in performing satisfactory validity studies; it will also include some who have been conducting good and fair selection programs and may even have reasonable validation data to offer. The hardship and expense of defense against a lawsuit will persuade many to simply give in – either to applied pressure or in anticipation of future pressures.

Yet, although the short-term outlook for test use is somewhat less than rosy, the longer term vista is more optimistic. When the EEOC was first created, we at The Psychological Corporation were delighted. We had been begging industry for many years to give proper attention to validity studies – begging with very little result. One of the outcomes of EEOC activities has been the forced recognition by those who want to retain their testing programs that validation is necessary. Every professional must rejoice that some companies are finally going to devote the time and effort required to investigate validity; this aspect of the personnel function is now getting long overdue attention.

The pressure on the publisher should be beneficial too. The instruments he prepares will have to satisfy more stringent requirements. Items will have to be selected for less irrelevant cultural variance as well as for criterion-relatedness. Attention will have to be paid to the characteristics of the total potential work force, not just to a majority of that force. It is reasonable to expect that the effect of attending to these added requirements will be to improve the validity of the tests – for blacks and whites alike.

We may also hope that many of the bad tests now infesting the industrial scene will be eliminated as a result of scrutiny stimulated by EEOC. There are too many "home-made" tests around – some made in the home of a personnel manager, some prepared in the kitchen of an industrial consultant. Most such tests could not withstand close scrutiny and should be consigned to oblivion. Like the society offenders on KoKo's list, they might well be underground and they'd none of them be missed.

As we chase out bad tests, we will be impelled to accelerate the search for good new tests. This may take the form of developing increasing numbers of what Cronbach has called narrow bandwidth, high fidelity instruments – tests aimed at very specific abilities. It may take the form of seeking new kinds of measures of the individual. Robert Glaser has suggested that there are "new aptitudes" which would be more predictive of ways of learning different from those we have heretofore been engaged with. If there are such new aptitudes, they should lend themselves to measurement just as our present traditional aptitudes do. In any event, a search for new approaches and new dimensions should be salutary.

I am optimistic that when affairs have finally shaken out, there will be more industrial testing rather than less. When it becomes evident, as it eventually will, that dropping tests does not remove vulnerability – that the interview and the application form must also be defended – I expect a return to testing as the most objective and indeed the most defensible selection procedure. Even if a company seeks to protect itself by adopting a quota system of hiring (despite the Supreme Court's admonition), there will be a need to identify the more likely among the applicants. Nothing else will serve this purpose as well as tests.

It is my conviction too that as blacks receive the better education to which they are entitled, more of them will be better prepared to perform on the job – whatever that job may be. As they find their fair place in our economy, there will be less talk of differential prediction; there will be less pressure from commissions and courts. The business of appraising people will continue, because the need will continue. And tests will remain the fairest and best means of appraisal.

I am certain I have neglected to mention some aspects of the responsibilities of the publisher of employment tests because I have taken them for granted or felt them to be implicit in my other remarks. I am confident my colleagues here assembled will be not only willing but positively eager to bring these omissions to my attention. I know I have not fully discussed the roles the publisher must play; in part, at least, this is a function of time. I will close with a simple summary statement. For this professional publisher, the publication of tests is the occasion for him to demonstrate his professional competence and his professional conscience.

Testing and Counseling:
Fact and Fancy

At the APGA Convention of 1971, Leo Goldman delivered a paper entitled "Tests and Counseling: The Marriage That Failed" (see Measurement and Evaluation in Guidance, 1972, 4, 213-220). The following year in Chicago, a number of Dr. Goldman's colleagues gathered in a symposium to argue that the marriage either had not failed or could be saved, each according to his particular view. One of these was Alexander G. Wesman. This paper was his rejoinder.

As a preamble let me say that I quarrel with Leo Goldman as my friend – though, I believe, a misguided one. I agree with him and with my fellow panel members that tests can and should be improved. I also agree that we as authors and publishers have a responsibility to work for improved test usage. I firmly believe, however, that the primary responsibility for proper test usage in counseling rests with the counselor and the counselor-trainer.

The opportunity offered me today was to defend the Differential Aptitude Tests (DAT) from the charge that they are of little value in the counseling process. As author and publisher of these tests, I find the temptation considerable to talk about the DAT for as long as I am permitted. As Leo Goldman said in the AMEG luncheon speech, I am one of those authors, publishers, and editors, "mostly nice people," who "are deeply involved with their test," who "believe in it," and who "have sweated over it."

What I vehemently deny is that I am a doting parent, not "as tough-mindedly realistic about the child's limitations as other people are." I submit that if we are highly professional people, as that same speech acknowledges, we know more about the values and the limitations of our instruments than do those for whom our instruments are simply one more tool; for to us tests are a matter of full-time attention. The best test constructors know more about the weaknesses of tests, and their strengths, than do less well-informed critics. The most professional, and therefore most responsible, test authors acknowledge those deficiencies as they acknowledge the merits of tests.

Accordingly, I will not argue for the contributions of DAT to counseling or plead once more for more intelligent use of DAT scores by counselors. I would hope that the recognition granted to DAT by the Council of Guid-

From *Measurement and Evaluation in Guidance*, 1972, 5, 397-402. Copyright 1972 American Personnel and Guidance Association. Reprinted with permission.

ance and Personnel Associations (APGA's predecessor) in bestowing one of its first research awards on this battery, the singling out of DAT by Quinn McNemar in his American Psychological Association (APA) presidential address as the best instrument of its kind, the year-to-year utilization of the tests by so many guidance departments over the last two decades, despite the fact that we have not had salesmen or regional offices to push the tests – all these factors should adequately affirm that DAT needs no special defense.

What is needed now is a rejoinder to the charges addressed to tests in general by Leo Goldman in his 1971 AMEG luncheon address, "Tests and Counseling: The Marriage That Failed."

Tests as a Counseling Tool

The marriage metaphor used to describe the relationship between counseling and tests was obviously meant to be provocative, and some of us found it provoking. If one were to reply in kind, one might suggest that it is not divorce that is being proposed – it is murder and suicide. The rejection of tests as useless or harmful is an attempt to kill them off; but for the counselor to do without the information tests can provide would in many circumstances be suicide. I seriously doubt that the educational profession or society would give the same support to counselors who offer only warmth and nondirective reflection as they have given to counselors who combine these qualities with hard facts about student abilities.

It would be a mistake, however, to pursue the literary flight of fantasy treating tests and counselors as mates in marriage; enough mischief has already been perpetrated by this unfortunate and inappropriate bit of anthropomorphism. The author has apparently himself been led astray by his whimsy. Counselors are indeed people, but tests are not – tests are merely tools. As with all other tools, some tests are better made than others, some have more versatile applications, and all are subject to proper use, misuse, abuse, and neglect. The workman who uses a screwdriver instead of a chisel should not criticize the manufacturer of the screwdriver; the counselor who misuses tests should not fault the tests.

Nor is it accurate for Goldman to say that makers of tests have sought to dominate the counseling process. One of the most persistent themes in testing literature has been the importance of using tests as only one of many sources of information about a counselee. A counselor who has failed to learn this principle is either ill-prepared in testing and counseling or is simply too lazy to do his job properly. In either case it hardly seems reasonable to lay all of the blame at testing's door; it might better be shared by the counselor and counselor-trainer.

Test authors and publishers believe what good counselors believe – information obtained from well-chosen and properly interpreted tests, when integrated with all other relevant information about a student that a counselor can obtain, will improve the quality of the service the counselor gives and the decision the counselee makes.

Perspective on Prediction

Let us examine next the charge that test scores are so undependable, so imprecise as to make them virtually useless in the counseling process. A first, annoyed rejoinder might be to ask about the dependability and predictive validity of other information the counselor uses. How valid for prediction is the counseling interview when test data are unavailable? How predictive are anecdotal records, or references? How comparable are grades from class to class and school to school? But there is a less contentious, more direct reply that can be made, and this is to draw attention to more fruitful uses of the statistical formulas that led Leo Goldman to abandon tests as imprecise and therefore of little value.

It is inevitable, I suppose, that this argument about precision will crop up every now and again when new members of the profession confront tables of bivariate distributions. I had hoped to clarify the matter for some colleagues in 1953, when I wrote a Test Service Bulletin entitled "Better Than Chance," for over 100,000 readers (Wesman, 1953). Copies are still available without charge for those who want them. Let me quote from that document.

> In most practical work, such precision is unnecessary. We do not ordinarily need to predict that John Jones will be exactly at the 85th percentile in a college class, or that Bill Smith will be 19th in a group of 25 engineering apprentices. We are far more likely to be concerned with whether Jones will survive the first year in college, or whether Smith will be one of the satisfactory apprentices. For these purposes, whether Jones is at the 75th percentile or the 90th percentile is of lesser moment; we can make a quite confident prediction that he will succeed, even though there may be a fair-sized standard error of estimate applicable to the specific percentile our formula predicts.

> A second factor working in our favor in the practical use of tests is that... predictions are most accurately made at the extremes – and it is the extremes that are of greatest interest to us. Few colleges grant large scholarships to more than 10 or 20 per cent of their students. Few colleges fail as many as half their students and few industrial firms fire as many as half of those they hire. More often, the failures are 10 per cent or 20 per cent or possibly 30 per cent – the extremes. Thus a test which does not predict with accuracy whether students will be at the 40th percentile or the 60th percentile can still do a valuable service in predicting that very few of the high scorers will be in the 20 per cent who fail during the freshman year, or that hardly any scholarship winners will be academic failures. In industrial selec-

tion, a test of moderate validity can be efficient in quickly screening out the "clearly ineligible" from the "clearly eligible." There will remain an indifferent zone of test scores for persons in the "eligible" range; for them, other considerations than test scores may determine whether they should be hired [pp. 9-10].

Copies of Test Service Bulletins on simple and double-entry expectancy tables – or experience tables if you prefer – are also available (Wesman, 1949, 1966). I was happy to have Goldman join those of us (mostly test authors) who have encouraged their use over the years. Of course, we cannot be highly optimistic that this plea will meet with uniform success either. Although I prepared my original article on the subject in 1949, I was a johnny-come-lately even then: Edward L. Thorndike and Walter Van Dyke Bingham advocated their use several decades earlier. Let us hope that the time has finally arrived for widespread use of these tables. As our earliest DAT manuals documented, validity is specific to school, grade, and subject; and as those manuals maintained, the preparation of local expectancy tables is valuable both for understanding the nature of prediction in the local situation and for explaining the meaning of correlation to students, parents, and administrators. I applaud Goldman's efforts in support of this cause.

My applause is more restrained regarding Goldman's confessions of sin over computers – especially since he appears to be implicating the testing field in his sinning. (This portion of Goldman's 1971 luncheon address was cut from the article that appeared later in *MEG*.) His disappointment in the contribution of computers is unfortunate if inevitable, but it is hardly the fault of tests that his expectations were ingenuous.

Computers will respond only with the input they have received – with test data from test experts or with counselors' interpretations if computers are to be used for counseling purposes. If the counselor writes a library of interpretive statements that are naive or unfounded, the computer will spew them forth. If the counselor prepares a more reasonable library, the computer will provide extraordinarily rapid printouts of those more warranted statements.

To look for computer interpretations from outside the realm of its input would truly be fantastic. It would make more sense to recognize that the computer has at least two excellent gifts to offer. The first is the ability to manage enormous amounts of data. The second is the ability to make available to run-of-the-mill medical practitioners interpretations of information (such as MMPI profiles) from experts like those in the Mayo Clinic and to offer run-of-the-mill counselors the interpretations of information (such as DAT scores plus biographical data plus stated vocational plans) from people like Super or Thompson or Wrenn or Berdie or Layton or Tiedeman – perhaps even Leo Goldman. When counselors learn better how to interpret all kinds of information and feed that new body of knowledge and wisdom to the computer, only then will it be reasonable to expect improved counseling from a computer.

Testing and the Disadvantaged

Let us look next at the criticism of tests used with the disadvantaged. In his luncheon address Goldman said, "It is almost impossible to conceive of a test which does not demand understanding of one or more concepts." This should be followed by the statement, "It is entirely impossible to conceive of a curriculum or a learning situation which does not demand understanding of concepts." Our present tests measure curriculum-relevant aspects of what an individual has learned; accordingly they predict what the individual is likely to learn. This need not be attributed, as Goldman attributes it, to the gloomy (though perhaps realistic) expectation that the prediction is accurate for the disadvantaged because they will continue to be disadvantaged. It can be attributed to a realistic view of how learning progresses – what one knows at the present forms a basis for what one can proceed to learn.

This principle holds true no matter what curriculum may be devised; it is as true for learning Swahili as it is for learning French. If the curriculum were radically changed, we might need different tests to do as good a job of prediction as our current tests do – but they would still measure concepts, percepts, the ability to make certain kinds of discriminations, for these abilities are fundamental to all learning. If a child has not learned needed concepts, percepts, or discriminations, it may not be his fault – but he is handicapped just the same. We cannot effectively help him if we are ignorant of his handicaps.

Goldman's general attack on tests as unfair to disadvantaged pupils is too far-ranging to be susceptible to a full response on this occasion. A task force of the American Psychological Association addressed itself over a period of many months to the problems of employment testing of minority groups; it did not reach Goldman's conclusions (APA Task Force on Employment Testing of Minority Groups, 1969). A report prepared for APA by a similar committee which studied the educational use of tests with the disadvantaged will soon be forthcoming; it too has not reached Goldman's conclusions. Yet the broad goals of these studies and Goldman's criticism are the same – to help cure the ills of a society whose conscience has all too recently been awakened.

The essential difference is that Goldman proposes that we do without tests. The committees I have mentioned believe that to do so would deprive us of vital information. As the APA report on employment testing stated,

The ideal of full conservation of human resources demands careful appraisal of the current capabilities of individuals in our society. Only by learning as much as possible about each person's relevant job skills, knowledges, and aptitudes can his special individuality be used in the optimum possible way for himself and for his society. Thus, individual appraisal is crucial as a means of differentiating from among a group those persons who have attributes particularly well suited for doing certain jobs or tasks, or those for whom specialized training may be particularly suitable [p. 648].

Unfair discrimination in the world of work is a serious social ailment. In a sense, poor showing on tests may be one of many symptoms of this ailment. It is clear, however, that careful, informed, and judicious use of tests to aid in making personnel decisions can be essentially a positive rather than a negative action toward persons with backgrounds of limited opportunity [p. 649].

You don't cure malnutrition by throwing out the scale that identifies babies who are underweight. You don't win a war by killing the messenger who brings news of defeat in a skirmish. If tests reveal that the disadvantaged have been deprived of opportunities to learn fundamental concepts, the remedy is to provide those opportunities – not do away with the source of information. If it is true that minority children do not have the motivation to learn, as Goldman suggests, we should work toward instilling that motivation and not pretend (by neglecting to test) that they actually have learned, thus dooming them to future failure to learn.

To make tests the scapegoat for the ills of the disadvantaged is not only unfair to test publishers and authors, it is unfair to a society that needs to know and to grow. I believe that given the proper setting in which to learn – at school, in the home, in the everyday world – blacks, Chicanos, Indians, and Puerto Ricans can earn their way to the status they properly seek. They *can* learn and, given the proper learning opportunities, they can demonstrate this learning on the kinds of tests that we have today. It is short-sighted to state that we can have black physicians and physicists only if we don't require that they be well trained. Give them the opportunity to learn and you won't need to be afraid of how they will score on tests – they'll score well.

Summary

I have not addressed myself to those aspects of Goldman's speech that deal with data. These are covered to a considerable extent in the reports to which I have alluded. I am here discussing a philosophy – one that is of great importance. The remedy for the ills of society is not to dispense with diagnosis; it is to treat the ills.

I suppose the best way of summarizing my remarks is to say, quite simply, that test data represent information – and I am deeply convinced that professionals do their jobs better with information than without it. I cannot accept the proposition that the solution to the problems of society is ignorance of facts. We must know what we are, if we are to know what we can become.

References

American Psychological Association Task Force on Employment Testing of Minority Groups. Job testing and the disadvantaged. *American Psychologist,* 1969, *24,* 637-650.

Wesman, A.G. Expectancy tables: A way of interpreting test validity. *Test Service Bulletin No. 38.* New York: The Psychological Corporation, 1949.

Wesman, A.G. Better than chance. *Test Service Bulletin No. 45.* New York: The Psychological Corporation, 1953.

Wesman, A.G. Double-entry expectancy tables. *Test Service Bulletin No. 56.* New York: The Psychological Corporation, 1966.

Bibliography

The comparative efficiency of various methods of weighting interest test items. *Psychological Bulletin*, 1939, *36*, 569-570. (With R. T. Rock, Jr.)

Consistency in response and logical interpretation of psychoneurotic inventory items. *Journal of Educational Psychology*, 1941, *32*, 321-338. (With P. Eisenberg)

The perception of relationship in human adults. *Journal of Experimental Psychology*, 1941, *28*, 63-76. (With P. Eisenberg)

A progress report of the committee on basic concepts in biology. *Graduate Record Examination Occasional Circular* (No. 2). New York: Carnegie Foundation for the Advancement of Teaching, 1943. (With W. Etkin, F. R. Kille, & L. G. Livingston)

A progress report on the sophomore-senior achievement of 383 twice-tested college students of liberal arts. *Graduate Record Examination Occasional Circular* (No. 1). New York: Carnegie Foundation for the Advancement of Teaching, 1943.

Test scores of honors students. *Graduate Record Examination Occasional Circular* (No. 3). New York: Carnegie Foundation for the Advancement of Teaching, 1944.

A study of transfer of training from high school subjects to intelligence (Doctoral dissertation). *Teachers College, Columbia University Contributions to Education* (No. 909), 1945. Summary of dissertation in *Journal of Educational Research*, 1945, *39*, 254-264.

Personnel Classification Test. New York: Psychological Corporation, 1946 (Form A), 1947 (Form B), 1964 (Form C). Manual 1947, 1948 (Rev. ed.), 1951 (Rev. ed.), 1965 (Rev. ed.).

The use of "none of these" as an option in test construction. *Journal of Educational Psychology*, 1946, *37*, 541-549. (With G. K. Bennett)

The usefulness of correctly spelled words in a spelling test. *Journal of Educational Psychology*, 1946, *37*, 242-246.

Active versus blank responses to multiple-choice items. *Journal of Educational Psychology*, 1947, *38*, 89-95.

Differential Aptitude Tests. New York: Psychological Corporation, 1947 (Forms A & B), 1962 (Forms L & M), 1972 (Forms S & T). Manual 1947, 1952 (2nd ed.), 1959 (3rd ed.), 1966 (4th ed.), 1974 (5th ed.). (With G. K. Bennett & H. G. Seashore)

Industrial test norms for a southern plant population. *Journal of Applied Psychology*, 1947, *31*, 241-246. (With G. K. Bennett)

The Differential Aptitude Tests: Some comments by the authors. *Occupations*, 1948, *27*, 20-22. (With G. K. Bennett & H. G. Seashore)

Needed: More understanding of present tests. *Improving Educational Research*. Washington, D.C.: American Educational Research Association, 1948, pp. 63-68.

What is an aptitude? *Test Service Bulletin* (No. 36). New York: Psychological Corporation, 1948.

Aptitude testing for differential prediction. *Growing Points in Educational Research*. Washington, D.C.: American Educational Research Association, 1949, pp. 187-193.

Effect of speed on item-test correlation coefficients. *Educational and Psychological Measurement*, 1949, *9*, 51-57.

Expectancy tables—A way of interpreting test validity. *Test Service Bulletin* (No. 38). New York: Psychological Corporation, 1949.

Frequency vs. complexity of words in verbal measurement. *Journal of Educational Psychology*, 1949, *40*, 395-404. (With H. G. Seashore)

Separation of sex groups in test reporting. *Journal of Educational Psychology*, 1949, *40*, 223-229.

Verbal factors. *Proceedings of the 1948 Invitational Conference on Testing Problems*. Princeton, N.J.: Educational Testing Service, 1949, pp. 52-53.

The standardization of the Wechsler Intelligence Scale for Children. *Journal of Consulting Psychology*, 1950, *14*, 99-110. (With H. G. Seashore & J. E. Doppelt)

The three-legged coefficient. *Test Service Bulletin* (No. 40). New York: Psychological Corporation, 1950.

Counseling from profiles—A casebook for the Differential Aptitude Tests. New York: Psychological Corporation, 1951. (With G. K. Bennett & H. G. Seashore)

Guidance testing. *Occupations*, 1951, *30*, 10-14.

Problems of differential prediction. *Educational and Psychological Measurement*, 1951, *11*, 265-272. (With G. K. Bennett)

Aptitude testing: Does it "prove out" in counseling practice? *Occupations*, 1952, *30*, 584-593. (With G. K. Bennett & H. G. Seashore)

The Differential Aptitude Tests—A five-year report. *Personnel and Guidance Journal*, 1952, *31*, 167-170.

The Differential Aptitude Tests as predictors of achievement test scores. *Journal of Educational Psychology*, 1952, *43*, 210-217. (With J. E. Doppelt)

An experimental comparison of test-retest and internal consistency estimates of reliability with speeded tests. *Journal of Educational Psychology*, 1952, *43*, 292-298. (With J. P. Kernan)

Faking personality test scores in a simulated employment situation. *Journal of Applied Psychology*, 1952, *36*, 112-113.

Personnel Tests for Industry. New York: Psychological Corporation, 1952 (Forms A & B), 1967 (Forms C & D). Manual 1954, 1969 (Rev. ed.). (With J. E. Doppelt)

Reliability and confidence. *Test Service Bulletin* (No. 44). New York: Psychological Corporation, 1952.

Better than chance. *Test Service Bulletin* (No. 45). New York: Psychological Corporation, 1953.

Review of Iowa Legal Aptitude Test. In O. K. Buros (Ed.), *The fourth mental measurements yearbook*. Highland Park, N.J.: Gryphon Press, 1953.

Review of Law School Admission Test. In O. K. Buros (Ed.), *The fourth mental measurements yearbook*. Highland Park, N.J.: Gryphon Press, 1953.

Standardizing an individual intelligence test on adults: Some problems. *Journal of Gerontology*, 1955, *10*, 216-219.

Aptitude, intelligence, and achievement. *Test Service Bulletin* (No. 51). New York: Psychological Corporation, 1956.

College Qualification Tests. New York: Psychological Corporation, 1956 (Forms A & B), 1959 (Form C). Manual 1957, 1961 (Rev. ed.). (With G. K. Bennett, M. G. Bennett, & W. L. Wallace)

The Differential Aptitude Tests: An overview. *Personnel and Guidance Journal*, 1956, *35*, 81-91. (With G. K. Bennett & H. G. Seashore)

Methods of identifying gifted students. *Guidance News*, October 1956, pp. 4-5.

The obligations of the test user. *Proceedings of the 1955 Invitational Conference on Testing Problems*. Princeton, N.J.: Educational Testing Service, 1956, pp. 60-65.

A test battery for teaching tests and measurements. *The 13th Yearbook of the National Council on Measurements Used in Education*, 1956, pp. 76-78.

Comparability vs. equivalence of test scores. *Test Service Bulletin* (No. 53). New York: Psychological Corporation, 1958.

Multiple regression vs. simple addition of scores in prediction of college grades. *Educational and Psychological Measurement*, 1959, *19*, 243-246. (With G. K. Bennett)

Review of Medical College Admission Test. In O. K. Buros (Ed.), *The fifth mental measurements yearbook*. Highland Park, N.J.: Gryphon Press, 1959.

Review of Scholastic Mental Ability Tests. In O. K. Buros (Ed.), *The fifth mental measurements yearbook*. Highland Park, N.J.: Gryphon Press, 1959.

What kinds of tests for college admission and scholarship programs? *Proceedings of the 1958 Invitational Conference on Testing Problems*. Princeton, N.J.: Educational Testing Service, 1959, pp. 114-120.

NDEA: Opportunities and responsibilities in test development and test use. *Personnel and Guidance Journal*, 1960, *39*, 41-44.

Review of *Essentials of Psychological Testing* by L. J. Cronbach. *Science*, April 22, 1960, pp. 1209-1210.

Some effects of speed in test use. *Educational and Psychological Measurement*, 1960, *20*, 267-274.

Academic Promise Tests. New York: Psychological Corporation, 1961 (Forms A & B). Manual 1961, 1962 (Rev. ed.), 1965 (Rev. ed.). (With G. K. Bennett, M. G. Bennett, D. M. Clendenen, J. E. Doppelt, J. H. Ricks, Jr., & H. G. Seashore)

Introduction to symposium: Standard scores for aptitude and achievement tests. *Educational and Psychological Measurement*, 1962, *22*, 5-6.

Preface. *Proceedings of the 1963 Invitational Conference on Testing Problems*. Princeton, N.J.: Educational Testing Service, 1964, pp. v-vii.

Testing for differential aptitudes. *Educational Horizons* (official publication of Pi Lambda Theta), 1964, *43*, 31-36.

Review of Iowa Tests of Educational Development. In O. K. Buros (Ed.), *The sixth mental measurements yearbook*. Highland Park, N.J.: Gryphon Press, 1965.

Review of National Educational Development Tests. In O. K. Buros (Ed.), *The sixth mental measurements yearbook.* Highland Park, N.J.: Gryphon Press, 1965.

Double-entry expectancy tables. *Test Service Bulletin* (No. 56). New York: Psychological Corporation, 1966.

Emphatically different (Review of *Educational measurements and their interpretation* by F. B. Davis). *Contemporary Psychology*, 1966, *11*, 132; 134.

Intelligent testing. *American Psychologist*, 1968, 23, 267-274.

Job testing and the disadvantaged. *American Psychologist*, 1969, *24*, 637-650. (With B. Baxter, D. W. Bray, A. Carp, M. Dunnette, R. L. Ebel, & S. J. Messick—members of APA Task Force on Employment Testing of Minority Groups)

Writing the test item. In R. L. Thorndike (Ed.), *Educational measurement* (2nd ed.). Washington, D.C.: American Council on Education, 1971.

No tribute to the colonies (Review of *Assessing intellectual ability* by B. A. Akhurst). *Contemporary Psychology*, 1972, *17*, 400.

Review of Advanced Placement Examinations. In O. K. Buros (Ed.), *The seventh mental measurements yearbook* (Vol. 2). Highland Park, N.J.: Gryphon Press, 1972.

The role of the publisher with respect to testing for employment purposes. In K. E. Clark (Chair), *Conference on the Use of Psychological Tests in Employment (Particularly with Minority Group Members).* Conference at University of Rochester, Rochester, N.Y., 1972.

Testing and counseling: Fact and fancy. Presented at *Symposium: Tests and Counseling*, American Personnel and Guidance Association, Chicago, 1972. Also in *Measurement and Evaluation in Guidance*, 1972, 5, 397-402.

Educational uses of tests with disadvantaged students. *American Psychologist*, 1975, *30*, 15-41. (With T. A. Cleary, L. G. Humphreys, & S. A. Kendrick—members of Ad Hoc Committee on Educational Uses of Tests with Disadvantaged Students, appointed by APA's Board of Scientific Affairs)

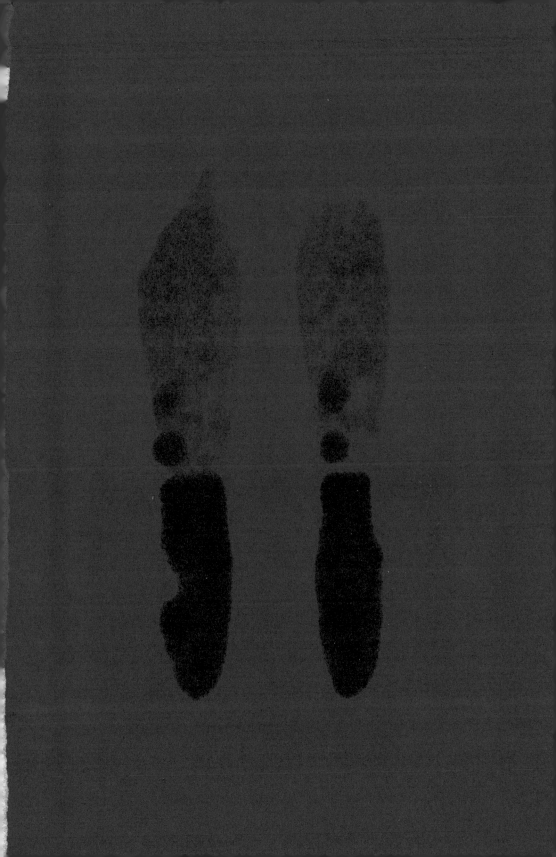

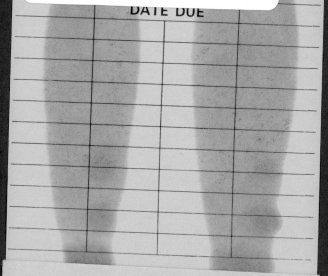